The
Child Abuse
Doctors

STM **Learning**, Inc.

Leading Publisher of Scientific, Technical, and Medical Educational Resources

St. Louis

www.stmlearning.com

i

Our Mission

To become the world leader in publishing and

information services on child abuse,

maltreatment, diseases, and domestic violence.

We seek to heighten awareness of these issues

and provide relevant information to

professionals and consumers.

*A portion of our profits is contributed to nonprofit organizations
dedicated to the prevention of child abuse and the care of victims
of abuse and other children and family charities.*

This book is dedicated to my wife, Michele Chadwick whose love, devotion and
day-to-day care made it possible and whose insights gave it perspective.

David L. Chadwick, MD

The
Child Abuse
Doctors

David Chadwick, MD
Director Emeritus
Center for Child Protection
Children's Hospital – San Diego
Adjunct Associate Professor
Graduate School of Public Health
San Diego State University
San Diego, California

STM **Learning**, Inc.

Leading Publisher of Scientific, Technical, and Medical Educational Resources
St. Louis
www.stmlearning.com

Publishers: Glenn E. Whaley and Marianne V. Whaley
Design Director: Glenn E. Whaley
Managing Editor: Sharifa N. Barakat
Associate Editor: Mallory C. Skinner
Book Design/Page Layout: G.W. Graphics
                              Heather N. Green
Print/Production Coordinator: Heather N. Green
Cover Design: G.W. Graphics
Developmental Editor: Sharifa N. Barakat
Copy Editor: Mallory C. Skinner

Printed in the United States of America

Publisher:
STM Learning, Inc.
609 East Lockwood Ave., Suite 203 St. Louis, Missouri 63119-3287 USA
Phone: (314)993-2728 Fax: (314)993-2281 Toll Free: (800)600-0330
http://www.stmlearning.com

Library of Congress Cataloging-in-Publication Data

Chadwick, David L.
  The child abuse doctors / David Chadwick.
     p. ; cm.
  Includes bibliographical references.
  ISBN 978-1-878060-69-3
  1. Abused children--Medical care. 2. Abused children--Medical care--
History. I. Title.
  [DNLM: 1. Child Abuse. 2. Child Abuse--history. 3. Pediatrics. 4.
Physicians. WA 325]
  RJ375.C45 2011
  362.76--dc22
                                        2010030155

Foreword

As early as 900 BCE, the Persian physician Rhazes, who practiced in the harems of Baghdad, described intentional injury to children. Soranus, a Greek gynecologist of the second century AD, advocated for infanticide in babies who were "born early, who lack a vigorous cry" and who are not "perfect in all parts." In 1559, Ambroise Pare, the famous French surgeon, wrote the first description of subdural hematoma as the consequence of trauma. Paulus Zachias, a "doctor from Rome and a most distinguished gentleman" reported on "disastrous head injury in children from beating" in 1651. In 1800, James Parkinson of London wrote that head injury as consequence of "disciplining" may result in intracerebral hemorrhage and hydrocephalus.

The most famous of early describers of child abuse was Auguste Ambroise Tardieu (1818-1879) who recorded the largest series of child abuse fatalities and the most comprehensive description of child maltreatment in all of its medical manifestations in 1860. Less well-known was the description in 1930 by Sherwood, who described 9 cases of subdural hematoma in which there was a question of possible trauma with no admission and Ingraham and Matson, who, in 1944, considered trauma likely to be an etiologic factor in head injury. Eleven of the cases they described had fractured skulls and they described retinal hemorrhages.

In this comprehensive and highly accessible book on the medical history of child abuse, Chadwick has made a landmark contribution. Beginning with Tardieu and continuing through to the present day, he has recorded the evolution of the recognition of child abuse.

Because of dedication and conviction, countless physicians have labored intensively, often against great odds, to provide scientific validation to the diagnosis of child abuse. Initial denial—within the community at large as well as in the medical establishment—was gradually replaced with realization that abuse does occur all too frequently. *The Child Abuse Doctors* documents this tumultuous history of doctors' attempts to protect children from abuse. It is an essential work for any medical professional interested in working in child abuse pediatrics.

A pioneer in his own right, having made numerous contributions to the medical literature and establishing the Chadwick Center at San Diego Children's Hospital, Chadwick's deep involvement in the field of child abuse medicine gives credence to this text. This monograph will be invaluable for future generations of medical professionals charged with the recognition, treatment, and prevention of child abuse.

Robert M. Reece, MD

Clinical Professor of Pediatrics
Tufts University School of Medicine
Director
Child Protection Program
The Floating Hospital for Children
Tufts New England Medical Center
Boston, Massachusetts
Editor
The Quarterly Update
North Falmouth, Massachusetts

FOREWORD

This is a book about altruism. The provision of clinical care and the conduct of research in child abuse are among the most difficult career paths available to physicians or other health care providers. Other areas in health care are far more likely to result in grateful families and patients, reasonable hours, peer recognition, incomes comparable to peers, access to research support, and professional advancement. To colleagues, the child abuse clinician is a savior who relieves them of the difficult call, the unpleasant interaction with family, and the onerous duty to come to the foreign territory of the court system to testify as needed. All of us who work in this area hear the phrase "I don't know how you can do this work" almost daily.

The clinicians who work in this area have a few secrets. First, the majority of cases that we deal with are neglect, and these families benefit greatly from the attention and intervention of the medical care system and are often quite welcoming of the help of a physician who can move mountains to call attention to their plight. Second, the other professionals who work with these families are appreciative and peer recognition helps replace the absent relationship that other physicians have with their patients and families. Third, child abuse pediatrics is an intellectually stimulating form of medical practice as the clinician has to carefully consider the plausibility of alternative hypotheses, think carefully about the biomechanics, differential diagnoses, and even the epidemiology of injury. Fourth, the interface of health care, law, social services, and cultural norms and practices is a fascinating place to work and learn about improving the human condition. And finally, we get to work with kids who are still, through most of it, kids. They can be funny and exasperating, and we can improve their lives. In response to the "I don't know how..." phrase, one can respond that no medical subspecialty has patients that all do well and that the prognosis for our patients may well be the best among our subspecialty colleagues. Good, careful, and early work can correct the social circumstances that lead to the maltreatment, and the majority of child maltreatment victims will have normal lives. The reward for this investment can mute the emotional difficulty of hearing each child's individual story and seeing their pain.

The attractant to the field has always been interpersonal relationships. Mentors and role models, with whom we developed relationships in residency training or medical school, led most of us to this field. The biographies in this volume are testimony to the power of mentoring. Much of the mentoring has addressed clinical care and how to work with all of the systems involved. Mentoring in maltreatment research is a rarer commodity; the number of physicians who have secured National Institute of Health support to work on aspects of maltreatment is small. Whereas other fields have benefited from a lab culture with a cadre of senior investigators sharing the nuances and approaches needed in a field, the absence of the National Institutes of Health in this field for almost a generation has deprived it of a senior brain trust of researchers who know how to secure federal research support. That needs to be fixed. The biographies presented here include some of the pioneers who have begun to crash that world.

Give due regard to the wisdom of the author; Dr. David Chadwick is a giant in this field. His work has spanned this field from its earliest days with C. Henry Kempe to seminal research on the epidemiology of falls and injury in young children, to recent efforts to involve public health systems. He has been a leader in pushing public health to monitor the occurrence of child abuse and neglect, in developing interdisciplinary evaluations, in developing standards of care and inculcating science into medical conclusions, and in building a constituency of survivors and their families to speak forcefully on the need for prevention. The historical and clinical perspective here gives ample evidence to the force of altruism.

Desmond K. Runyan, MD, DrPH

Professor of Social Medicine & Pediatrics
University of North Carolina School of Medicine
National Program Director
Robert Wood Johnson Foundation Clinical Scholars Program
Chapel Hill, North Carolina

Preface

In 2006, Robert Block described the founding of a new subspecialty in *Pediatrics* named Child Abuse Pediatrics. This announcement followed decades of developmental work in medicine in general and in pediatrics in particular and focused on the ways in which physicians might provide useful services that would prevent child abuse or ameliorate its health harms. About 20 years earlier, I had begun to work full-time as a child abuse doctor based in a Children's Hospital. With the successful definition of the subspecialty in pediatrics, I realized that I had been a close-up witness to the development of this field and, perhaps, I should write something to describe my own experiences. Many colleagues supported this notion, and I produced an outline. STM Learning, Inc. also provided encouragement and this book became a reality.

C. Henry Kempe is prominently featured in this monograph for describing physical abuse in a way that put an end to further evasion when he named a new condition "The Battered Child Syndrome." Kempe having been a professor of mine at the University of California, San Francisco, we remained in touch, and he invited me to participate in a meeting to draft the model child abuse reporting law. Not long before, I had been dragged, kicking and screaming, into the child abuse field by Los Angeles social worker Helen Boardman. Although I was more interested in infectious diseases, Boardman insisted that I provide careful medical assessments and, sometimes, testimony on infants and children who were appearing at the Children's Hospital of Los Angeles with multiple, poorly-explained injuries. In 1968, I moved from Los Angeles to San Diego and assumed the position of Medical Director at the Children's Hospital in San Diego.

In the 1970s, San Diego was already fertile ground for the development of child abuse programs. The police department in the city had a specialized child abuse unit, and a legendary social worker, Elizabeth Lennon, was working to coordinate the efforts of all of the public agencies in the city and the county of San Diego. Around 1975, a transplant from Kempe's program in Colorado, Diana Bryson, arrived in the city and volunteered to help build a child abuse program at the Children's Hospital. By 1980, a well-developed multifaceted child abuse program was in place at the Children's Hospital in San Diego, and, in 1985, it was possible for the program to be made a hospital department and for me to assume the directorship of the Center for Child Protection.

Meanwhile, throughout the US, more and more medical doctors were becoming interested in child abuse, and we were able to prevail on the American Academy of Pediatrics to establish a committee and a specialty section to focus on the problem of child abuse. San Diego was on the child abuse map, and I was well-positioned to see what was going on throughout the country. Other doctors in other locations undoubtedly have somewhat differing views of this history. Still, the contents of this book are as accurate as I can make them. They are eyewitness testimony.

There are various themes that are emphasized in The Child Abuse Doctors. The importance of child abuse as a health problem is obvious, but it is equally obvious that a sufficient understanding of the phenomenon and an attempt to reduce its health harms must require the application of knowledge from a variety of disciplines and professional sectors. These include sociology and social work; psychology and psychiatry; anthropology; and law and criminal justice. In dealing with individual cases, it is essential to use teams, representing different disciplines and different agencies that can intervene appropriately and stop ongoing abuse or apply appropriate sanctions after the fact. The salient importance of the "health sector" for successful dealing with child maltreatment is a theme of this book.

Another prominent theme of the book is the value of child abuse doctors. Child abuse doctors are important contributors to the health of society and that they make their contributions in the face of daunting difficulties. Although they make up only a tiny fraction of the medical profession, they are making a significant impact on the problem of the many health harms caused by child maltreatment. They have often been supported by children's hospitals and by pediatric departments in medical schools despite a severe shortage of governmental or other forms of external support for their programs. It is the child abuse doctors themselves who have invented, codified, and legitimized a new medical specialty and discipline.

More doctors in the US have specialized in child abuse than in any other country, and my direct knowledge about their experiences is largely confined to the US. Individual stories of child abuse doctors are included in this book. To some extent, the stories are determined by my selection, and some of the content is contributed by the individuals. However, I take responsibility for all content in this book, including any details in the doctors' stories.

Writing this book has been a revelatory experience. I hope that the history it contains will provide a foundation for medical doctors and health professions to make an effective effort to eliminate child maltreatment. Our history to this point tells us that the health system has the best chance of accomplishing this goal.

David L. Chadwick, MD

TABLE OF CONTENTS

The
Child Abuse
Doctors

STM **Learning**, Inc.

Leading Publisher of Scientific, Technical, and Medical Educational Resources
St. Louis
www.stmlearning.com

THE FIRST PUBLISHED MEDICAL RECOGNITION OF CHILD ABUSE: THE WORK OF AUGUSTE AMBROISE TARDIEU

Auguste Ambroise Tardieu was the most prominent forensic pathologist of the mid-19th century as well as the first doctor of medicine to systematically describe the anatomical effects of both physical and sexual abuse of children,[1-3] publishing details of 32 cases in 1860. His descriptions of the changes produced by physical abuse, sexual abuse, and extreme neglect anticipated many observations made in the 20th century. Although the descriptive term was not yet coined, he identified subdural hematomas resulting from inflicted head injuries. Before the advent and use of x-rays, Tardieu described fractures and explained patterns of bruising that could not be accidental. He described severe genital injuries, some of which were accompanied by histories of rape, and opined that the injuries could be indicative of rape for legal purposes.

Although Tardieu's work cited earlier case reports by Toulmouche and others,[1] he was the first to point out that the problem was prevalent and could be diagnosed by a doctor of medicine in living children by physical examination and by autopsy after death. Tardieu was famous in his own time, but not because of his description of the pathology of child abuse. He wrote a textbook on toxicology, published numerous articles on many aspects of forensic pathology, studied and testified about notorious French murder cases. At the University of Paris, the world center of medical learning in the mid-19th century, Tardieu served as a faculty member. There is no record of any contemporary contradiction of his conclusions, but there is no record of supplementation or extension either.

Jeffrey Masson[4] writes that Sigmund Freud must have learned about the work of Tardieu when Freud went to Paris to study with Jean-Martin Charcot. Freud's personal library contained Tardieu's book describing child sexual abuse, but he never mentioned Tardieu in his writings.[4] Freud argued that histories of sexual abuse provided by children and adult "hysterics" were actually fantasies, and his argument appears to have overridden the anatomical evidence documented by the pathologist. There was a mindset that child abuse was rare, and Freud added credence to it. In any case, doctors generally did not continue to explore the medical issues discovered by Tardieu.

Tardieu described outcomes of criminal prosecutions in child abuse cases,[3] and by his account, he provided expert testimony in such cases. He may have been the first and the last medical doctor to formally bear witness to child abuse in legal proceedings until 1965 when Theodore Curphey wrote in *California Medicine*, challenging medical examiners to document the injuries of battered children who died.[5] This author can recall testimony by pediatricians and radiologists in the early 1960s and by pathologists, such as Curphey, soon afterward. Although he decried criminal prosecution, in 1968, Ray E. Helfer[6] pointed out the importance of physicians' testimonies in criminal and protective legal proceedings.

Societies tend to resist and block out accurate descriptions of child abuse. Erna Olafson described these tendencies as "cycles of suppression,"[7] but the suppression may be more constant than cyclic. The phenomenon was already evident in the 19th century and affected the work of Tardieu. This theme and issue will be explored more in later chapters.

REFERENCES

1. Labbe J. Ambroise Tardieu: the man and his work on child maltreatment a century before Kempe. *Child Abuse Negl.* 2005;29(4):311-324.

2. Roche AJ, et al. The work of Ambroise Tardieu: the first definitive description of child abuse. *Child Abuse Negl.* 2005;29(4):325-334.

3. Tardieu A. Etude medico-legale sur les sevices et mauvais traitments exerces sur les enfants. *Annales d'Hygiene Publique et Medecin Legale.* 1860;13:361-398.

4. Masson JM. *The Assault on Truth: Freud's Suppression of the Seduction Theory.* New York, NY: Ballantine Books; 2003.

5. Curphey TJ, et al. The Battered Child Syndrome. Responsibilities of the Pathologist. *Calif Med.* 1965;102:102-104.

6. Helfer RE, Kempe CH8. *The Battered Child.* Chicago, IL: University of Chicago Press; 1968:43-58.

7. Olafson E, Corwin DL, Summit RC. Modern history of child sexual abuse awareness: cycles of discovery and suppression. *Child Abuse Negl.* 1993;17(1):7-24.

Chapter 2

THE SILENT CENTURY, 1860-1950

After Auguste Ambroise Tardieu's contributions, the only recorded 19th-century venture into the child abuse field by a medical doctor was Sigmund Freud's paper on the etiology of hysteria, which was presented to an audience of Vienna psychiatrists in late 1896. However, the Victorian-era novelists Victor Hugo and Charles Dickens appeared aware of child maltreatment, and both described it vividly—if incompletely—in their novels. This chapter describes the 19th-century events that led to a later child protection movement and to the emergence of child abuse doctors.

FREUD'S RECANTATION: HOW FREUD MISLED MEDICINE, PSYCHIATRY, AND PSYCHOLOGY AND DELAYED THE RECOGNITION OF THE IMPORTANCE OF CHILD ABUSE

Two thoroughly researched books document the facts that, in 1896, Freud had accumulated details of 18 cases in which women with "hysteria" (patterned psychosomatic symptoms) had provided him with histories of childhood sexual abuse, often by their fathers or other persons close to them or their families.[1,2] Both Jeffrey Masson and Florence Rush provide documentation that Freud presented a paper to the Psychiatric Society of Vienna in 1896, and that he described these cases in detail and built a theory that child sexual abuse or "seduction" was the cause of the condition then known as "hysteria." The 2 authors use the same source documents as their bases for these facts, and they rely mainly upon the letters written by Freud to Wilhelm Fliess.

Both authors agree that Freud later recanted his "seduction theory" and replaced it with the theory that the women had fantasized the abuse. Freud theorized that these fantasies were traumatic to the women and resulted in their psychosomatic symptoms later in life. However, they differ about Freud's reasons for revising his theory. Masson attributes the recantation to extreme pressure from other members of the Psychiatric Society as well as Freud's Viennese friends and relations, many of whom might have been personally involved in some of the cases. Rush points out that other aspects of Freud's work were highly controversial, especially his views on religion and sex, making it unlikely he would have recanted because of social pressures. Instead, she suggests the recantation stems from personal motives, relating to Freud's early childhood and his relationships within his family. Given the exhaustive work of these 2 authors and the many other psychiatrists and historians that have examined the archival material, it is unlikely that more light can be shed on the reasons behind Freud's alteration of his theory. Freud himself never spoke directly to this question.

Judith Herman[3] emphasizes the brilliance, insight, and logic that is found in Freud's paper on "The Etiology of Hysteria." Freud published this work in 1896,[1,4] and reading it a century after it was delivered and in the light of 20th-century research, this author agrees with Herman's assessment. Freud published this lecture in German, and it was later translated and republished by James Strachey,[5] and an English version is published as an appendix in Masson's book, *The Assault on Truth*.[1]

Whatever his reasons, Freud's recantation of the "seduction theory" has had a profound effect on psychiatry, psychology, medicine, and sociology. While the recognition and description of physical abuse was the province of pathologists, general practitioners, and pediatricians, the recognition and description of sexual abuse should have been the province of psychiatrists and psychologists, dealing with the secondary mental health problems that are now known to be produced by such abuse. To estimate the number of persons whose sexual abuse went unrecognized as a result of Freud's influence is impossible; however, the renunciation of his original theory produced incalculable harm. Mental health conditions, such as posttraumatic stress disorder, that result from sexual abuse went undiagnosed and untreated because of the failure of professionals to accept the likelihood of its occurrence. His recantation forced the field to rediscover child sexual abuse.[5]

Despite his tortured theory on hysteria, Freud's great influence in the field of psychology and other disciplines is generally well deserved because of the value of his contributions, especially his recognition of unconscious influences on feelings and behaviors. He also pioneered the recovery of memories lost due to developmental memory failure or to suppression by pain. One cannot help but wonder what accomplishments might have been achieved had he stuck to his guns in 1897.

Additional harm has come about because of society's reluctance to accept the notion children may often be abused by persons who should be protecting them. This tolerance of abuse still permeates society, and to some extent, it facilitates the backlash[6] against professionals, including child abuse doctors, who attempt to deal with child maltreatment in an effective way.

19TH-CENTURY STIRRINGS

THE BIRTH OF PEDIATRICS: HOW THE EXISTENCE OF DOCTORS FOR CHILDREN FACILITATED THE RECOGNITION OF CHILD ABUSE

Advances in public health and a decline in infant mortality in the 19th and early 20th centuries were associated with the development of the medical specialty of pediatrics. In earlier eras, in which more than half of infants died before their first birthdays, parents could not set a high value on individual children. In the 19th century, the valuation of children increased. The existence of pediatricians and an increasing regard for the well-being of children, together, facilitated the recognition of child abuse by doctors.

NOVELISTS AND JOURNALISTS: HUGO, DICKENS, AND RIIS

Although most doctors and other well-educated and advantaged persons in the 19th century chose not to write about child abuse, novelists Hugo and Dickens described it in their literature. As commercial writers of fiction, Hugo and Dickens depended on readership for their livelihoods; therefore, their writings did not dwell explicitly on unpleasant realities. Still, both of them managed to convey some of the problems affecting children in the 19th century.

Hugo wrote a poem about child labor that depicts the exploitation of children. In a translated excerpt, Hugo writes,

Where do these children go for whom nobody laughs?
These sweet, pensive beings wasted away by fever?
These eight year-old girls you see walking alone?
They go to work - fifteen hours in the mill;
They go from dawn to dusk, eternally repeating
The same motions in the same prison.
Stooped beneath the teeth of a somber machine.

In *Les Miserables*[7] Hugo describes the plight of an orphaned girl placed in what passes for foster care but more closely resembles indentured servitude, and he also describes the lives of Paris street children, or *gamins*. He applies a romantic gloss to his description, which is a way to avoid offending his readership with too much reality.

In *Oliver Twist*,[8] Dickens portrays the lives of poor and orphaned children in England. The stable of London boys controlled by the sinister character Fagin is a vivid example of exploitation, although a contemporary reader will suspect that Dickens has only told about half that story. In *Bleak House*, he tells the story of an orphaned girl cared for by distant relatives, and in passing, he vividly depicts the death of a newborn baby on its mother's lap in a hovel with no aid or comfort of any kind. These authors influenced their readers to become more conscious of the plight of many poor children and their families. Some readers might have recognized the novelists' descriptions to be reality-based and been influenced to undertake social or political change.

MARY ELLEN

The case of Mary Ellen occurred in New York at the end of the 19th century, and it was described in detail by investigative journalist Jacob Riis.[9] It involved a young girl who was orphaned and cared for by a substitute family and subjected to repeated and severe physical abuse. Her rescue was facilitated by an attorney who was a board member of the Society for the Prevention of Cruelty to Animals. Subsequently, that society became the American Humane Association and became concerned with the welfare of children as well as dogs and cats. The case received very extensive public attention, and the result was a substantial increase in both public and private social resources to support poor children and their families.

In the 100 years following 1860, medical doctors continued to ignore child abuse and its resultant physical and mental health problems, but a number of things happened that facilitated doctors' concerns that would develop in the 20th century. Public health was born around 1850, and one of its effects was to allow the survival of many more infants and young children so that parents could increase their emotional and economic investments in their offspring.

In addition, in the 19th century, women began to reach out for more rights and more security. Because most care of children was provided by women, the development of feminism led to better protection for children. Though it would take many decades, the stage was being set for the medical recognition of child abuse.

REFERENCES

1. Masson JM. *The Assault on Truth: Freud's Suppression of the Seduction Theory*. New York, NY: Ballantine Books; 2003.

2. Rush F. A Freudian Cover-Up. In: Rush F, ed. *The Best Kept Secret: Sexual Abuse of Children*. New York, NY: McGraw-Hill; 1981:80-104.

3. Herman JL. *Trauma and Recovery: The Aftermath of Violence—From Domestic Abuse to Political Terror*. New York, NY: Basic Books; 1997:7-14.

4. Freud S. L'hérédité et l'étiologie des névroses. *Revue Neurologique*. 1896;4:161-169.

5. Freud S. The Aetiology of Hysteria. In: J Strachey, ed. *The Standard Edition of the Complete Psychological Works of Sigmund Freud*. London: Hogarth Press; 1953.

6. Hechler D. *The Battle and the Backlash: The Child Sexual Abuse War*. Lexington, MA: Lexington Books; 1988.

7. Hugo VM. *Les Miserables*. New York, NY: Modern Library; 1992.

8. Dickens C. *Oliver Twist*. New York, NY: The Heritage Press; 1940.

9. Riis J. The Story of Mary Ellen. In: Riis J, ed. *The Children of the Poor*. New York, NY: Putnam; 1894.

Chapter 3

THE MEDICAL REDISCOVERY OF PHYSICAL ABUSE BY C. HENRY KEMPE

C. Henry Kempe personally rediscovered child physical abuse in the 20th century; however, prior to his 1962 publication of "The Battered Child Syndrome,"[1] 2 other doctors had observed the problem but failed to name it. Both John Caffey, in 1946, and Frederick Silverman, in 1953, had written painstakingly detailed descriptions of cases involving coincidental bone and head injuries, and Silverman emphasized that the bone lesions he saw were caused by physical injuries, but neither drew the conclusion that these injuries stemmed from child abuse.

In 1962, Kempe's published work directly attributed these types of injuries to child abuse and paved the way for general recognition of the problem. In this process, he became the first child abuse doctor.

JOHN CAFFEY: AN ABUNDANCE OF CAUTION

In 1946, Caffey published a series of 6 cases of infants with chronic subdural hematomas in association with multiple fractures. None of the infants had a history of an injurious event.[2] Caffey considered a number of possible causes for the fractures and the associated subdural hematomas, but abstained from concluding that the infants had been intentionally injured. Thus, Caffey, in an abundance of caution, avoided any conclusion that would imply abusive behavior by the parents of the injured infants. This avoidance was typical of most medical doctors at that time.

Caffey achieved many notable things. He established the specialty of pediatric radiology and was the first doctor to describe radiological findings in previously under-studied conditions, such as scurvy and rickets, and to recognize many conditions that had not been described previously. A consummate academic physician, he published the first textbook of pediatric radiology, *Pediatric X-Ray Diagnosis*, in 1945. Taking his achievements into account, his blindness to the possibility of serious physical abuse by parents was not due to a lack of medical knowledge or acumen,

9

but was typical of medical doctors of the times due to concern about legal repercussions.

Regardless of his reluctance to implicate the parents of injured children, Caffey's meticulous descriptions of the cases are still worth reading. Because of the era in which he practiced, he was familiar with nutritional deficiencies and discounted rickets and scurvy, bone conditions that might mimic fractures, as causes of injuries.

In 1972 and 1974, Caffey named shaken baby syndrome,[3,4] a serious and frequently fatal form of abusive head injury, first described by A.N. Guthkelch.[5]

One of Caffey's accomplishments was the training of many young pediatric radiologists. Silverman was prominent among them. He provided further insight into the types of injuries Caffey had described in 1946.

SILVERMAN'S SYNDROME AN EVANESCENT EPONYM

In 1953, Silverman published an article describing 3 cases of what he called "unrecognized trauma."[6] These cases were classified as such because the infants demonstrated bone abnormalities he was certain were due to injury, but which generally had been attributed to other causes or left unexplained. Silverman used the terms "metaphyseal rarefaction," "metaphyseal infraction," and "periosteal new bone formation" to describe lesions he believed were caused by manual traction on extremities. The pediatricians and orthopedists who had examined the infants and ordered x-rays to be taken did not consider the lesions to be injuries, so Silverman conducted his own interviews with the parents. This was very unusual for a radiologist, who would normally see the x-rays of a child, but would not interview the parents. In 2 cases, Silverman obtained histories of accidental injuries that he believed were consistent with the bodily damage he observed. Two years later, Paul V. Woolley[7] published an article based on observations of similar cases, but took a firmer stand that the children's caregivers inflicted the injuries.

Silverman gave lectures about these strange injuries and, in one such talk, referenced Auguste Ambroise Tardieu's 19th-century work in Paris. He implied that the injuries were usually of abusive origin and suggested the eponym, Tardieu's syndrome, naming the condition after the first doctor to describe medical findings of child abuse. A French professor of pediatrics attended the lecture and later suggested the problem of abusive injuries be referred to as Silverman's syndrome. Neither name caught on.

Forty years later, in a solicited letter to the *Journal of Pediatric Radiology*, Silverman[8] stated that both he and Caffey believed the injuries they had reported had been inflicted by the children's parents; however, neither doctor was willing to put that belief into print and submit it for peer review and publication. Caffey was concerned about the possible legal repercussions of alleging abuse.

Blindness to child abuse was difficult to overcome and was the rule, rather than the exception, in the medical profession. Caution was not simply abundant; it was intellectually stifling.

C. HENRY KEMPE: AN END TO EVASION

In this climate of uncertainty and avoidance, Kempe described and defined child physical abuse in a manner that would make evasion difficult and captured the attention of the medical profession **(Figure 3-1)**. Because Kempe was the respected chairman of a pediatric department and active in the American Academy of Pediatrics (AAP), he was able to present a plenary session titled "The Battered Child Syndrome" at an annual meeting of the AAP in 1961, ensuring him a large and influential audience. The session comprised a panel discussion of cases by Kempe, Brandt Steele, and Silverman. Some doctors criticized the session as "overly dramatic," though the existence of a "syndrome" of physical abuse has never been seriously challenged. A short time later, Kempe published an article with the same title in the *Journal of the American Medical Association*.

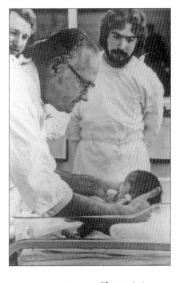

The biography[9] of Kempe—written by his daughter—documents some of the difficulties he encountered while trying to gain acceptance for his presentation of "The Battered Child Syndrome." The provocative title was adopted despite concern that most pediatricians would not attend a presentation about abused children. In the months following the presentation, Kempe received many critical comments from doctors who argued that child physical abuse did not occur in the manner he described. Most of them based their denials of Kempe's descriptions on the fact they had never seen such a case, and Kempe typically responded that they had, indeed, seen the condition but had failed to recognize it.

Figure 3-1.
C. Henry Kempe
on the left.

Kempe's firm and public stand did not just receive harsh criticism; it attracted unwanted attention in the form of threats. In his biography, Annie Kempe describes her father receiving a death threat via a telephone call to their home. While such threats to child abuse doctors are uncommon, they occur often enough to bespeak a climate of hostility to persons who intervene to protect children. Still, Kempe was undeterred and continued to treat and study child abuse.

This author and a number of colleagues had seen cases similar to those described by Kempe, Caffey, and Silverman and welcomed Kempe's ground-breaking publication. For example, Vincent Fontana, who provided medical care for abandoned infants at the New York Foundling Hospital, where he saw many abused children, quickly chimed in with an article, "The Child Maltreatment Syndrome" in 1963. The number of articles about child abuse in the indexed medical literature jumped from 5 in 1962 to 100 in 1967 and over 200 in 1970.

"THE BATTERED CHILD SYNDROME" ARTICLE OPENED THE DOOR

Kempe's "The Battered Child Syndrome" summarizes medical findings in hundreds of cases of abuse across the US, many of them observed in the 2 Denver hospitals affiliated with his pediatric department. Co-authored by Silverman, who described similar cases in 1953; Steele, a psychiatrist who evaluated many of the parents of the abused children seen in the Denver hospitals; and William Droegemueller and Henry Silver, associates of Kempe's, the article emphasizes the significance of fractures and notes that, in most of the documented cases, the histories provided failed to justify the injuries sustained.

Kempe pointed out that, while many cases of abuse showed signs of repeated injuries over a substantial period of time, others showed only a single occurrence of injury. He observed that many of the affected infants died and suggested recognition and intervention could be protective, while failure to intervene could prove fatal.

In "The Battered Child Syndrome," Steele's detailed studies of the parents of battered infants and children indicated that such abuse was often generational. Steele also observed that abusive parents were rarely psychotic and did not generally fall into standard psychiatric diagnostic categories. Steele and social worker Elizabeth Davoren developed close relationships with parents who had inflicted serious injuries on their children, gaining insight into the parents' lives and the dynamics of their abusive behaviors. Steele and Davoren tried to rationalize the parents' behavior, analyzing the motives that prompted the abuse. They found that many abusive parents had been abused themselves. In some cases, Steele and Davoren believed they could ensure the safety of the young children in their own homes, but, in others, they could not, depending on the parents' acceptance of support.

THE EFFECTS OF "THE BATTERED CHILD SYNDROME" ARTICLE

Kempe's article has had profound and lasting effects. Most 20th-century writings about child abuse have cited "The Battered Child Syndrome," and many attribute the awakening of society and professionals in the fields of health, social services, and criminal justice to a consciousness of the problem to the work of Kempe and his associates. The article paved the way for additional medical articles written in the late 20th and early 21st centuries. Kempe knocked down the barrier that had restrained doctors from writing about child abuse in the preceding century. In addition, the term "battered child syndrome" gained legal credence, and in recent decades judges have generally allowed physicians to testify to its occurrence in order to establish the fact that a child has been abused.[10] Finally, the publication of "The Battered Child Syndrome" was the catalyst for the development of medical centers that provide services for child abuse, where doctors could focus on the problem. The definition of a medical syndrome of child abuse led to the possibility of child abuse doctors in the same way that studies on heart disease led to the medical specialty of cardiology.

The article and its echoes also affected the course of Kempe's career. Until 1962 and for some time afterward, he had been sub-specializing in infectious diseases, concentrating on smallpox, and had taken a leadership role in the global effort to eradicate that plague. The effort was successful, and Kempe refocused his energy onto child abuse. Indeed, most of his speaking and writing after 1962 was about child maltreatment.

CONFIRMATORY WORK

At about the same time Kempe was publishing, 2 social workers published articles that described families with similar problems. Elizabeth Elmer,[11] in Pittsburgh, and Helen Boardman,[12] in Los Angeles, published articles. Boardman's article was supported by an article, written by John Gwinn,[13] a Los Angeles pediatric radiologist.

THE FIRST BOOK: THE BATTERED CHILD

Among his many achievements, Kempe initiated the first comprehensive book about child abuse titled *The Battered Child*.[14] Kempe quickly realized that no one discipline could—or should—attempt to deal with the complex subject of child abuse unaided, and he recruited authors from pediatrics, psychiatry, sociology, law, law

Figure 3-2.
Karl Heinz Kempe in Hitler's Germany, circa 1932. Image provided by Annie Kempe.

enforcement, and social work to contribute to the book. *The Battered Child* was the first book to be published that set guidelines and standards for all of the professions that encountered child abuse.

KEMPE'S UNIQUE ACHIEVEMENT

A look at Kempe's personal history may explain his motivation to publish clear definitions of child abuse at a time when others found it impossible to do so. Kempe grew up a German Jew in Breslau, in what was then eastern Germany, during Hitler's rise **(Figure 3-2)**. His parents fled to South America, and he escaped to England and later the US, but because of widespread denial of the genocide happening in Europe, many of his relatives and friends perished in the Holocaust. Therefore, Kempe was well aware of the danger of denial of abusive practices, and was strongly motivated to illuminate the reality of child abuse. The important thing was not the discovery of abuse, but the courage to name it.

THEORIES OF THE ORIGINS OF PHYSICAL ABUSE: SOCIOLOGISTS' CONTRIBUTIONS

While Kempe and the researchers in Denver theorized that physical abuse was generational, with abused children growing up to become abusive parents, sociologist David Gil took a broader view, theorizing the stresses of poverty and a cultural acceptance of physically punishing children were the underlying causes of child abuse.[15-17] Gil urged that reducing incidents of child abuse required renewed efforts to lessen the impact of poverty and cultural changes in the use of corporal punishment. Gil based his theory on an extensive national survey he conducted using reported cases of child abuse and a data collection instrument administered by the social workers who had investigated the cases. He employed a causal typology of physical child abuse that considered circumstances immediate to the abuse as observed by the social workers. The most common circumstance leading to physical abuse was disciplinary action taken to correct a child's disobedient behavior. However, Gil's typology included a number of other circumstances, including "sadistic impulses" in the perpetrators. Eighteen percent of the cases Gil surveyed involved abuse by a perpetrator who experienced a sadistic impulse.[17] During the year he spent at the Kempe Center, the British psychiatrist David Jones observed sadism in cases of physical abuse.[18]

In addition to surveying social workers who investigated reports of child abuse, Gil surveyed a small sample of the general public regarding their attitudes toward and knowledge of child abuse. From this sample, he inferred a general tolerance of the physical abuse of children. Many respondents indicated that they could understand how someone might impulsively abuse a child, and most favored voluntary over coercive interventions.

Some professionals argue that physical child abuse is strongly related to external and cultural factors, while some consider it linked to individual behaviors. Both theories can be supported, since cases of both types occur.

A CENTER IN DENVER

Starting in 1963, Kempe began building a center to support professionals from several disciplines who could work with children and families on the problem of child abuse. He was unable to house the program in either of the affiliated Denver hospitals, but he found an abandoned convent, rented it, and converted the nuns' tiny cells into offices for a growing staff. The C. Henry Kempe National Center for the Prevention and Treatment of Child Abuse at 1205 Oneida Street in Denver was the first center of its kind in the US, and programs modeled after it began cropping up in children's hospitals and medical schools.

THE CHILD PROTECTION TEAM

The Child Protection Team was one of the most important and influential of Kempe's innovations. With increasing recognition of cases of infant and child abuse in the Denver hospitals, Kempe decided to take advantage of information available from public health nurses, mental health professionals, and governmental investigative agencies, such as public social services and law enforcement. He used the information gleaned from the various agencies and disciplines to develop composite portraits of each case of abuse, with the goal that these portraits would lead to more informed decisions about intervention. Kempe introduced regular multidisciplinary, multi-agency meetings at which cases were discussed and information shared. Known as Child Protection Team (CPT) meetings, they usually took place at the hospital. The idea spread and has given rise to many publications.[19-31]

THE CHILD ABUSE REPORTING LAWS

Not long after the presentation at the AAP, Kempe, along with Katherine Bain and Katherine Oettinger of the US Children's Bureau, chaired a conference in Washington to write proposals for laws that would require physicians to report cases suspicious of child abuse (see *Chapter 7*). The group that came together included medical doctors, social workers, lawyers, and law enforcement officers. Over the course of 2 to 3 days, they devised a "model" child abuse reporting law. After some fine-tuning by lawyers, this model was made available to the states, all of which soon adopted reporting laws.

Although there have been many contributors from many disciplines who have added to the description of child abuse, Kempe was the one who ended the centuries-old habit of sweeping abuse under the rug. After his work, society no longer ignored the problem.

REFERENCES

1. Kempe CH, et al. The battered child syndrome. *JAMA*. 1962; 181(1):17-24.

2. Caffey J. Multiple fractures in the long bones of infants suffering from chronic subdural hematoma. *AJR*. 1946; 56(2):163-173.

3. Caffey J. On the theory and practice of shaking infants. Its potential residual effects of permanent brain damage and mental retardation. *Am J Dis Child*. 1972;124(2):161-169.

4. Caffey J. The whiplash shaken infant syndrome: manual shaking by the extremities with whiplash-induced intracranial and intraocular bleedings, linked with residual permanent brain damage and mental retardation. *Pediatrics*. 1974;54(4):396-403.

5. Guthkelch AN. Infantile subdural hematoma and its relationship to whiplash injuries. *Br Med J*. 1971;2:430-431.

6. Silverman FN. The roentgen manifestations of unrecognized skeletal trauma in infants. *AJR Radium Ther Nucl Med*. 1953;69(3):413-427.

7. Woolley PV, Evans WA. Significance of skeletal lesions in infants resembling those of traumatic origin. *JAMA*. 1955;158:530-543.

8. Silverman FN. Letter/Commentary. *Pediatr Radiol*. 1994; 24:541-542.

9. Kempe A. *A Good Knight for Children: C. Henry Kempe's Quest to Protect the Abused Child.* Booklocker; 2007.

10. Myers JEB. *Legal Issues in Child Abuse and Neglect.* Newbury Park, CA: Sage Publications; 1992.

11. Elmer E. Failure to thrive: role of the mother. *Pediatrics.* 1960;25:717-725.

12. Boardman H.E. Project to rescue children from inflicted injuries. *Soc Work.* 1962;7(1):43.

13. Gwinn JL, Lewin KW, Peterson HG Jr. Roentgenographic manifestations of unsuspected trauma in infants. *JAMA.* 1961;176:926-929.

14. Helfer RE, Kempe CH, eds. *The Battered Child.* Chicago, IL: University of Chicago Press; 1968.

15. Gil DG. Incidence of child abuse and the demographic characteristics of the persons involved. In: Helfer RE, Kempe CH, eds. *The Battered Child.* Chicago, IL: University of Chicago Press; 1968:10-39.

16. Gil DG. A sociocultural perspective on physical child abuse. *Child Welfare.* 1971;50(7):389-395.

17. Gil DG. *Violence Against Children: Physical Child Abuse in the United States.* Cambridge, MA: Harvard University Press; 1973.

18. Jones DP. The untreatable family. *Child Abuse Negl.* 1987; 11(3):409-420.

19. Abdoo DC, Bross DC, Sirotnak AP. The Golden Anniversary of the Child Protection Team: 50 years and going strong. *Caring for Our Future.* Spring 2008:1-4.

20. Arnold DH, et al. Availability and perceived competence of pediatricians to serve as child protection team medical consultants: a survey of practicing pediatricians. *South Med J.* 2005;98(4):423-428.

21. Benbenishty R, Chen W. Decision making by the child protection team of a medical center. *Health Soc Work.* 2003; 28(4):284-292.

22. Bross DC, et al. *The New Child Protection Team Handbook.* New York, NY: Garland Publishing, Inc; 1988:624.

23. Chen W, et al. Roundtable sessions of a Children's Hospital child protection team. *Psychiatr Serv.* 2008;59(6):693.

24. Clark SJ, Wilkinson DR. Decision making by the child protection team of a medical center. *Health Soc Work*. 2003; 28(4):322-323.

25. Demaurex CG. Role of pediatric psychiatry in a child protection team (CAN team du CHUV) [in French]. *Rev Med Suisse Romande*. 2001;121(7):503-505.

26. Jacobson M. Local realities: a frontier perspective on child protection team practice. *Child Welfare*. 2002;81(5):737-755.

27. Kempe CH, Schmitt BD. Cost analysis of the child protection team. *Pediatrics*. 1978; 61(2):328-329.

28. Pammer W, et al. Use of telehealth technology to extend child protection team services. *Pediatrics*. 2001;108(3):584-590.

29. Pascoe JM, et al. Violence in North Carolina families referred to a child protection team. *NC Med J*. 1981;42(1):35-37.

30. Schechter LF. The benefits of smallness: developing a model for an effective rural child protection team. *Child Welfare*. 1981; 60(3):131-147.

31. Thun-Hohenstein L. Interdisciplinary child protection team work in a hospital setting. *Eur J Pediatr*. 2006;165(6):402-407.

Chapter 4

CHILD ABUSE MEDICAL CENTERS

Before 1960, the idea of a child abuse program based in a medical center had not been introduced, but in 2008, 196 children's hospitals responded to a survey indicating that they provided specialized health services for child abuse.[1] Although children's hospitals vary in caseloads, services, and staffing, most provide some sort of specialized child abuse program. In 2009, there was still no formal system for accreditation of hospital-based child abuse services, although the Joint Commission on Accreditation of Healthcare Organizations attempts to ensure hospitals comply with state laws when reporting child abuse.

CHILD ABUSE: INTERVENTIONS AND SERVICES

The social services and justice sectors play important roles in the management of child abuse cases. Both these sectors exist in public entities such as states, counties, and cities. Only these governmental entities can exercise coercive interventions such as the arrest of offenders or the protection of children by involuntary out-of-home placement. However, the management of serious physical abuse cases usually begins in a hospital. Beginning in the 20th century, infants and children with serious injuries were brought to medical centers. Often these were hospitals operated by cities or counties and often by a university medical school as well. Therefore, the 20th-century recognition of child abuse began in medical centers.

Trauma systems organized by local government were pioneered by the county hospitals in Chicago and San Francisco. Throughout the US, these systems have continued to evolve over the years under the watchful eye of the American College of Surgeons, which established itself as the accrediting agency for trauma care. These systems link prehospital care with advanced and comprehensive hospital care as well as with prevention and public health approaches to the trauma problem.

The doctors and nurses in these medical centers were the first persons to be designated as mandated reporters of child abuse when the child abuse reporting laws were written in the 1960s; however, they recognized that they could not exercise coercive interventions, and they did not wish to become policemen or prosecutors. They did not want to share the growing unpopularity of public social services.

In addition to cases of serious physical abuse, many sexually abused children also surfaced in hospitals, especially in emergency departments. Inevitably, there was an overlap of investigative activity. The medical histories taken by nurses or doctors covered much of the same ground as the interviews of victims and witnesses conducted by law enforcement officers or social workers. This fact imposed a requirement for multidisciplinary teams and for careful sharing of information between individual professionals and their parent agencies.

The development of child advocacy centers (CAC) was an effort by the justice sector to provide essential services for child sexual abuse evaluation (see *Chapter 6*); however, the services provided were identical to those being provided in those hospitals that had developed special services for sexual abuse. The logical solution to this problem of possible duplication was set forth by Dr. Carolyn Levitt in St. Paul, Minnesota, who pointed out that hospitals could qualify as child advocacy centers and go through the same accreditation processes as the freestanding CACs. The financial support for CACs was largely derived from state or local law enforcement agencies. However, Levitt's model has not been widely adopted, and only about 20 of 600 CACs are in medical centers. It is still a good idea.

STANDARDS FOR A CHILD ABUSE MEDICAL CENTER

In past decades, child abuse medical centers have been largely self-defined, and there was still no published set of standards in 2009. A number of the services provided for child outpatients could also be provided in freestanding clinics or offices not connected to hospitals, but the core service of consultation for children, who have suffered serious physical abuse, cannot be separated from hospitals. The types of essential, included services were described in a manual[2] in 1996 and will be described later in this chapter. As the field of child abuse pediatrics expands, child abuse medical centers will likely develop a more definitive set of standards.

PROPOSED DEFINITION OF A CHILD ABUSE MEDICAL CENTER

Child abuse medical centers provide diagnostic, treatment, and prevention services for all forms of child maltreatment to a substantial population—usually one or more political subdivisions: state, county, city, or census tract. In addition to these services, centers offer a significant number of educational and research programs.

Sensible public policy requires child abuse medical centers to be accessible to the entire US population. Measured against this requirement, at present, the US is a long way from fulfilling the needs of abused children.

SUGGESTED STANDARDS
THREE BASIC AREAS OF SERVICE
In order to satisfy this provisional definition of a child abuse medical center, the center must provide services that fall into 3 basic categories: diagnosis and documentation, treatment, and prevention.

Diagnosis and Documentation
Diagnosis and documentation include the forensic medical work described in *Chapter 8*, as well as consultative examinations, the findings of which can be supported by expert reports and testimony. A child abuse medical center should be capable of diagnosing and documenting all forms of child maltreatment, including physical, emotional, and sexual abuse; neglect; and factitious illness produced by caregivers. In most centers, child abuse doctors primarily perform forensic work.

Treatment
Treatment includes the medical care and rehabilitation of physically injured children; the mental health care of children with emotional damage; and developmental enhancement programs for neglected infants and children. Treatments may involve a wide variety of professionals from trauma surgeons to psychotherapists, but all types of treatment should be available at child abuse medical centers.

Prevention
The prevention of child abuse requires the collaboration of workers from public health, social services, and a variety of personal health services. Although the prevention of child abuse is arguably a public health responsibility, very few state or local health departments provide preventive services. Rather, the most effective services for the prevention of physical child abuse and neglect are delivered in the home by nurses.[3] However, such programs can and should be administered by child abuse medical centers. A connection to perinatal care services is extremely valuable[4] because the most serious cases of physical abuse and neglect tend to occur very early in life.

THE FIRST CENTERS
COLORADO
C. Henry Kempe established the first health-based center for abused children and their families in the Department of Pediatrics at the University of Colorado School of Medicine. In that era, the Depart-

ment of Pediatrics was affiliated with 2 hospitals, the Colorado General Hospital and the Denver General Hospital, both public institutions. Neither hospital had space to house the growing Kempe National Center, so Kempe rented an abandoned convent and transformed the nuns' cells into offices. Although Kempe's initial emphasis was on the physical abuse cases treated at the 2 hospitals, he naturally gravitated toward abuse prevention, establishing family support services at the Kempe center. Members of the center's staff were also interested in the rehabilitation of physically abused and neglected infants and young children, and programs were established to serve that population.

Services for children who were sexually abused were also developed, and a number of publications about sexual abuse followed.[5,6] A half-century later, the Kempe National Center is still a major provider of education, services, and research regarding child maltreatment. The center is now affiliated with the Children's Hospital in Denver and is well described on a sophisticated Web site.[7]

WASHINGTON, DC
The Children's Hospital National Medical Center in Washington, DC was the second medical institution to establish a child abuse center, doing so in 1970. Associated with the George Washington University School of Medicine, the child abuse center was first led by Frederick C. Green[8-10] and later by Joyce N. Thomas, RN.[11,12] This center focused on child sexual abuse, and the staff contributed greatly to a compilation of practice guidelines published in 1980 by the National Center for Child Abuse and Neglect.[13] Thomas also initiated conferences, leading to the formation of the American Professional Society on the Abuse of Children (APSAC).

SEATTLE
Harborview Hospital in Seattle established a sexual assault center in 1971. At first, it focused only on services for adult rape victims who visited its emergency department, but with the arrival of the pioneer doctors, Shirley Anderson and John McCann in 1973, the hospital expanded its focus to include child sexual abuse victims. Anderson and McCann laid the groundwork for medical evaluations of sexually abused children.

The Harborview Hospital handled child physical abuse cases as well. Abraham Bergman and other staff members provided consultation on the child abuse cases in the early days, and more recently, the service has been provided by Kenneth Feldman and Naomi Sugar.

SAN DIEGO
Although child abuse cases were treated at the San Diego Children's Hospital for a number of years, the hospital did not designate a child

abuse center until 1976. In that year, the hospital implemented a prevention program with parents from the community volunteering to support the families of abused children. Services for sexually abused children, including skilled interviewing and medical examinations, were made available to the community in 1979. Within a few years, a program was added to provide mental health services to abused children and their families, and a comprehensive center was established. In 1985, this author became the full-time director of the Center for Child Protection at Children's Hospital–San Diego.

At that time, child abuse services in hospitals were growing around the country, but the idea of staffing the hospital's child abuse department with a full-time pediatric program director and sufficient personnel to service the city's nearly 2 million people was unique. It required the support of the hospital's chief executive officer, Blair Sadler, and a board of trustees with vision and understanding. The San Diego program is now known as the Chadwick Center for Children and Families at the Rady Children's Hospital and Health Center.

The first San Diego Conference on Child Maltreatment was held in 1986. The conference focused on health issues stemming from child maltreatment and attracted about 100 physicians and nurses. In later years, as many as 2000 child abuse professionals attended the conference annually.

Philadelphia

Inspired by Stephen Ludwig, as well as a large metropolitan population that brought many cases to the door, the Children's Hospital of Philadelphia (CHOP) developed focused child abuse services, beginning in 1980. Since then, CHOP has provided national leadership in many areas of child maltreatment. Although CHOP's services are comprehensive, the hospital has made notable advances in the research of inflicted head trauma.

At least 10 of the child abuse doctors who were active in 2009 trained at CHOP and were inspired by Ludwig. This contribution to education rivals that of Kempe and the University of Colorado, although it came much later in the history of the field.

Los Angeles and Pittsburgh

The National Association of Children's Hospitals and Related Institutions (NACHRI) recognizes the children's hospitals in Los Angeles and Pittsburgh as institutions that launched early child abuse programs. In fact, these 2 hospitals supported medical social workers, Helen Boardman and Elizabeth Elmer,[14-16] whose early writings about physical abuse and neglect confirmed many of

Kempe's observations. Although both hospitals developed protocol for dealing with cases of physical abuse and neglect, they did not have comprehensive child abuse programs until later.

Supporting Child Abuse Medical Centers

Hospital-based child medical centers struggle financially when their chief compensation comes from fee-for-service payments by for-profit insurance companies likely to refuse coverage for services to abused children. Very little useful information has been published about how to gain funding for child abuse medical centers. The experience of this author and several of his colleagues is that the managers and trustees of nonprofit hospitals can often be persuaded to subsidize child medical abuse programs because of the obvious value of the programs.

Some of the forensic medical work can be supported by contracts with local law enforcement or social service agencies. Fees for expert testimony by child abuse doctors can support forensic medical work; however, a physician's diagnosis and courtroom testimony require strict objectivity, and there can be no hint of financial advantage connected to the outcome of litigated cases. In fact, the American Medical Association Council on Judicial Affairs has ruled that linking compensation for expert testimony to the outcome of cases is unethical.[17]

There is strong evidence that mental health care for abused children and child prevention programs are cost-beneficial and might be supported using conventional fee-for-service arrangements. There is less evidence that criminal prosecution is cost-beneficial.

Grants or contracts from federal or state agencies become available periodically, and child abuse centers gain support from these sources. As the principal source of medical research funding, the National Institutes of Health has been minimally involved in supporting child abuse research.

At present, child abuse medical centers could be supported reasonably with federal or state public health funds on the grounds the centers will improve children's quality of life, reducing chronic illnesses attributable to child maltreatment. The system in the state of Florida, which provides "line-item" support for doctors and social workers to concentrate on child abuse in 21 of the state's hospitals, is the best in the country and could be replicated in other states.

Organizing and Managing Child Abuse Medical Centers

Child abuse medical centers should generally be directed by child abuse pediatricians because they have demonstrable qualifications and have qualified through an examination process. However, successful centers have been directed by psychiatrists, social workers, and nurses. Qualifications necessary for overseeing a child abuse medical center include a broad-based knowledge of child maltreatment, the management skills to make proper use of the resources at the center's disposal, and sufficient authority within a hospital or medical school.

EXISTING CHILD ABUSE MEDICAL CENTERS

In 2008, 196 children's hospitals responded to a survey indicating they provided specialized services for child abuse,[1] but currently, there is no strict definition of a center. The agency most capable of developing this directory and overseeing accreditation is the American Academy of Pediatrics; however, it is also a task that should be assumed by governmental public health agencies, such as the Centers for Disease Control. A formal system for accreditation is needed. The Joint Commission on Accreditation of Health Organizations has established a requirement that hospitals conform to existing state laws about the reporting of child abuse, but this requirement adds nothing, since all health providers are called out as "mandated reporters" and required by law to report child abuse.

There may currently be about 100 child abuse medical centers in the US that are worthy of that designation. The center in San Diego illustrates that, with proper staff and support, a single child abuse medical center can provide adequate service to a population of 3 million.

REFERENCES

1. National Association of Children's Hospitals and Related Institutions. *Responding to Child Maltreatment: 2008 Survey Findings and Trends.* Alexandria, VA: National Association of Children's Hospitals and Related Institutions; 2009.

2. Chadwick D. *Community Organization of Services Needed to Deal with Child Abuse,* in *APSAC Handbook on Child Maltreatment.* Myers J, eds. Thousand Oaks, CA: Sage Publications; 1996.

3. Olds DL. Prenatal and infancy home visiting by nurses: from randomized trials to community replication. *Prev Sci.* 2002: 3(3):153-172.

4. Olds DL, Sadler L, Kitzman H. Programs for parents of infants and toddlers: recent evidence from randomized trials. *J Child Psychol Psychiatry.* 2007;48(3-4):355-391.

5. Kempe R, Kempe CH. *The Common Secret: Sexual Abuse of Children and Adolescents*. New York, NY: W.H. Freeman & Company; 1984.

6. Kempe CH. Incidence of sexual abuse in the United States. *Child Abuse Negl*. 1984;8(3):377.

7. Kempe Center for the Prevention and Treatment of Child Abuse and Neglect. University of Colorado Denver Web site. http://www.uchsc.edu/peds/subs/kempe/faculty/index.htm. Accessed May 26, 2010.

8. Green FC. Child abuse and neglect. A priority problem for the private physician. *Pediatr Clin North Am*. 1975;22(2):329-339.

9. Green FC. Introduction: child sexual abuse: the physician's responsibility. *Pediatr Ann*. 1979;8(5):286-288.

10. Green FC. Human sexual aggression: social policy perspective. *Ann NY Acad Sci*. 1988; 528:400-403.

11. Thomas JN, Rogers CM. Sexual abuse of children: case finding and clinical assessment. *Nurs Clin North Am*. 1981;16(1):179-188.

12. Thomas, JN. Yes, you can help a sexually abused child. *RN*. 1980;43(8):23-29.

13. Jones BM, et al. *Sexual abuse of children: selected readings*. USDoHaH Services, OoHD Services, and YaF Administration for Children, eds. Washington, DC: US Government Printing Office; 1980.

14. Boardman HE. Project to rescue children from inflicted injuries. *Soc Work*. 1962;7(1):43.

15. Elmer E. Failure to thrive: role of the mother. *Pediatrics*. 1960;25:717-725.

16. Elmer E. *Fragile families, troubled children: the aftermath of infant trauma*. Pittsburgh, PA: University of Pittsburgh Press; 1977.

17. American Medical Association and Council on Ethical and Judicial Affairs. *Code of Medical Ethics: Current Opinions with Annotations*. Chicago, IL: American Medical Association; 1997.

Chapter 5

THE REDISCOVERY OF CHILD SEXUAL ABUSE

This chapter will describe how child sexual abuse was rediscovered in the 20th century following the long silence that was abetted by Sigmund Freud's theory that children's statements about abuse were fantasies. The rediscovery process was led by sociologists and not by medical doctors, although some of them joined in soon after the rediscovery began.

SOCIOLOGISTS LED THE WAY

Alfred Kinsey published one of the earliest and most important publications on the topic. In 1952, he reported that 24% of 1400 adult women remembered a pre-pubertal sexual experience with an older male.[1] Kinsey was attempting to examine human sexual behavior in a totally objective, scientific manner, and avoided terms, like "abuse," that implied judgment. The psychiatrist Lawrence S. Kubie[2] quickly pointed out that a behavior that was common was not necessarily moral or harmless. Like Christopher Columbus, Kinsey discovered something very important, but he didn't know what it was or how to correctly name it. His work illuminated a pathway that was followed by other sociologists in the 20th century who firmly established that child sexual abuse was common and harmful.

David Finkelhor contributed one of the early surveys of adults' recall of child sexual abuse,[3] and he summarized the progress in the early 20th century[4] through his book reviewing existing theories and proposing new theories. In this work, he deconstructed the reasons adults pursue sex with children, proposing 4 driving factors: emotional congruence with children, sexual arousal to children, blockage of sexual relationships with peers, and disinhibition. Disinhibition included the feminist theory that society generally tolerated sex between fathers and daughters among other circumstances.[5]

In 1983, Diana Russell conducted face-to-face interviews with about 1000 San Francisco women and found that 28% recalled sexual abuse occurring prior to 14 years of age.[6] These statistics were strikingly similar to those reported by Kinsey 30 years earlier.

There continues to be considerable variation in incidents of child sexual abuse attributable to definitions, survey methodology, and other artificial variables. However, research that began in the 1970s and 1980s exposed the pervasiveness of child sexual abuse. Since survey methods depended on recall of sexual abuse by the survey subjects, persons who were abused in infancy or early childhood could not reliably recall their abuse.[7]

EARLY CONTRIBUTIONS BY MEDICAL DOCTORS AND NURSES

Boston-based forensic nurse Ann Burgess[8-13] helped health professions to recognize the issue. She brought a mental health perspective to the problem of child sexual abuse. Suzanne Sgroi, a Hartford internist, followed Burgess, becoming the first medical doctor in the 20th century to publish substantial work on child sexual abuse.[14,15] Sgroi's *Handbook of Clinical Intervention in Child Sexual Abuse*,[16] published in 1982, remains an insightful and useful resource for multidisciplinary teams that intervene in cases of child sexual abuse. Drawing on the work of Burgess and Henry Giaretto,[17-19] Sgroi emphasized that the dynamic in child sexual abuse was more about power than sexual desire and that effective intervention and treatment of the perpetrators often—if not always—required the authority of the justice system. This issue was also explored by Alvin Rosenfeld and Eli Newberger,[20] who both argued for a balance between compassion and control.

In the *Handbook's* chapter on validation, Sgroi stresses the importance of skilled interviewing and devotes considerable space to providing detailed guidelines. She notes that, on genital examination, only a few sexually abused children have definite physical findings, but made a point of linking the occurrence of sexually transmitted diseases in children to the occurrence of sexual abuse.[21]

PSYCHIATRISTS RESPONDED SLOWLY

Freud's influence persisted powerfully in the 20th century, but a few intrepid psychiatrists published work pointing out that child sexual abuse was real and the cause of serious problems.[16-18] Roland Summit was the most influential of these pioneers,[22] and his landmark article on accommodation by child sexual abuse victims[23] clarified the problems of these children for professionals in all disciplines. He explained children's behaviors that had previously been attributed to their general unreliability or even malice and insisted that sexual abuse was an important cause of mental illness.[24] Because he was so influential, Summit was criticized by psychologists, like Ralph Underwager and Hollida Wakefield, who publicly contested accusations of abuse. As more child sexual abuse cases were tried in criminal and civil courts, attorneys defending abusers and their allies pressured potential witnesses for children with public attacks and threats of damage suits. Summit may have retired prematurely because of this pressure. Nevertheless, interventions in cases of child sexual abuse increased because of Summit's work.

SOCIAL WORKERS AND PSYCHOLOGISTS MADE MAJOR CONTRIBUTIONS

In 1980, Barbara Jones, Linda Jenstrom, and Kee MacFarlane were working at the US Children's Bureau and published a compilation of writings about child sexual abuse, *Sexual abuse of children: selected readings*, that described the state of knowledge and practice at that time.[25] Their work came at a time when literature on child sexual abuse was still sparse. It included writings by one of the medical doctors who pioneered the humane evaluation of child victims, Raylene De Vine. The compilation also contained the classic writing of Summit and JoAnn Kryso on "The Clinical Spectrum of Child Sexual Abuse." They noted, "The objective distinctions between loving support and lustful intrusion are disquietingly subtle."

MEDICAL EXAMINATION FOR THE DIAGNOSIS OF SEXUAL ABUSE

In the 19th century, Auguste Ambroise Tardieu[26] wrote about genital injury resulting from child sexual abuse, and a century later, medical doctors in the US revisited this idea. Wilmes Texeira, Bruce Woodling, and Astrid Heger[27] pioneered the use of magnified genital examination to reveal small injury lesions, raising hopes for increasing the sensitivity and specificity of the medical examination. However, these authors and others[28] noted that a knowledge base for normal examinations was lacking. The needed knowledge base required several years to develop, and over time, it became apparent that the contribution of the physical genital examination, although useful for forensic purposes in a minority of cases,[29] was usually less important than the history obtained by a skilled interviewer. This is because abuse can occur without much physical damage. It now appears that both methods—examinations and interviews—should be used whenever feasible.[30] Well-developed medical centers for abused children usually offer both approaches at the same site.[31]

THE IMPORTANCE OF SEXUAL ABUSE: THE DELINEATION OF HEALTH HARMS

As Freud's influence faded and victims' accounts of sexual abuse were increasingly accepted, the linkage of sexual abuse to mental and physical health problems was firmly established, although the extent of the connection is still being studied.[32] See *Chapter 7*.

Mental disorders resulting from severe stress or terror were mentioned by Herodotus and noted in many wars, but Judith Herman[33] and Bessel van der Kolk[34,35] were the modern pioneers who connected posttraumatic stress disorder (PTSD) to child sexual abuse. They argued that the problems of war veterans, captives, battered women, some persons affected by natural disasters, and sexually abused children all might enter the common symptomatic pathway now known as PTSD. This term can be expected to undergo further nosologic subdivision.

Medical centers for child abuse now typically offer mental health care specifically focused on the PTSD that results from child sexual abuse. Major improvements in this type of care have occurred over the last 3 decades.[36]

REDISCOVERY LED TO CONTROVERSY

The recognition of more cases of child sexual abuse inevitably led to an increasing number of interventions, some of which were necessarily coercive. These interventions led to litigation, which was always adversarial and became more so rapidly. The resulting turmoil in the 1980s is well summarized in David Hechler's book, *The Battle and the Backlash*.[37] Arguments against interventions in child sexual abuse cases took many forms. These included statements that sexual abuse didn't really exist except in the minds of therapists and social workers, that most allegations by children were false, or that sexual abuse was really harmless and that there were no adverse effects on children. The occurrence of cases that were incorrectly diagnosed or badly managed added fuel to the backlash fire. See *Chapter 9* for more information.

A general tendency in society to resist the revelation and the rational scientific study of child sexual abuse persisted into the 20th century, but the rediscovery was made by observers from different disciplines. This created a very different and more hopeful situation than the one faced by Freud in 1896. This time the toothpaste could not be squeezed back into the tube. Bitter court fights about individual cases still occur. Researchers also engage in harsh struggles over the elements of proof of abuse. Despite these issues, the recognition of the existence and scope of child sexual abuse is no longer an issue.

REFERENCES

1. Peters SD, Wyatt GE, Finkelhor D. Prevalence. In: Finkelhor D, Ed. *A Sourcebook on Child Sexual Abuse*. Beverly Hills, CA: Sage Publications; 1986:14-25.

2. Kubie LS. Psychiatric implications of the Kinsey report. *Psychosom Med.* 1948;10(2):95-106.

3. Finkelhor D. Sexually victimized children and their families. In: *Dissertation Abstracts International.* Ann Arbor, MI: ProQuest Information & Learning; 1979:7006-7007.

4. Finkelhor D, Araji S. *A Sourcebook on Child Sexual Abuse.* Beverly Hills, CA: Sage Publications; 1986:276.

5. Finkelhor D. *Child Sexual Abuse. New Theory and Research.* New York, NY: The Free Press; 1984.

6. Russell DE. The incidence and prevalence of intrafamilial and extrafamilial sexual abuse of female children. *Child Abuse Negl.* 1983;7(2):133-146.

7. Nelson CA. The nature of early memory. *Prev Med.* 1998; 27(2):172-179.

8. Burgess AW, Groth AN, McCausland MP. Child sex initiation rings. *Am J Orthopsychiatry.* 1981;51(1):110-119.

9. Burgess AW, Hartman CR. Children's adjustment 15 years after daycare abuse. *Forensic Nurs.* 2005;1(2):73-77, 83.

10. Burgess AW, et al. Response patterns in children and adolescents exploited through sex rings and pornography. *Am J Psychiatry.* 1984;141(5):656-662.

11. Burgess AW, McCausland MP. *Sexual exploitation of children through sex rings.* ANA Publ. 1979(NP-59):45-62.

12. Burgess AW, McCausland MP, Wolbert WA. Children's drawings as indicators of sexual trauma. *Perspect Psychiatr Care.* 1981;19(2):50-58.

13. Burgess EJ. Sexually abused children and their drawings. *Arch Psychiatr Nurs.* 1988;2(2):65-73.

14. Sgroi SM. Sexual molestation of children. The last frontier in child abuse. *Child Today.* 1975;4(3)18-21, 44.

15. Sgroi SM. Editorial: The abused child—physicians' obligations. *Conn Med.* 1975;39(7):418.

16. Sgroi S, ed. *Handbook of Clinical Intervention in Child Sexual Abuse.* Lexington, MA: Lexington Books; 1982.

17. Giarretto H. A comprehensive child sexual abuse treatment program. *Child Abuse Negl.* 1982;6(3):263-278.

18. Giarretto H. Community-based treatment of the incest family.

Psychiatric Clinics of North America. 1989;12(2):351-361.

19. Giarretto H, Einfeld-Giarretto A. Integrated treatment: The self-help factor. In: Horton AL, et al, eds. *The incest perpetrator: A family member no one wants to treat.* Thousand Oaks, CA: Sage Publications, Inc; 1990:219-226.

20. Rosenfeld AA, Newberger EH. Compassion vs control. Conceptual and practical pitfalls in the broadened definition of child abuse. *JAMA.* 1977;237(19):2086-2088.

21. Sgroi SM. Pediatric gonorrhea beyond infancy. *Pediatr Ann.* 1979;8(5):326-336.

22. Summit R, Kryso J. Sexual abuse of children: a clinical spectrum. *Am J Orthopsychiatry.* 1978;48(2):237-251.

23. Summit RC. The child sexual abuse accommodation syndrome. *Child Abuse Negl.* 1983;7(2):177-193.

24. Summit RC. The centrality of victimization. Regaining the focal point of recovery for survivors of child sexual abuse. *Psychiatr Clin North Am.* 1989;12(2):413-430.

25. Jones BM, et al. *Sexual abuse of children: selected readings.* USDoHaH. Services, OoHD Services, YaF Administration for Children, eds. Washington, DC: US Government Printing Office; 1980.

26. Tardieu A. *Étude médico-légale sur les attentats aux mœurs.* Paris, FR: Librairie JB Baillière et Fils; 1857.

27. Woodling BA, Heger A. The use of the colposcope in the diagnosis of sexual abuse in the pediatric age group. *Child Abuse Negl.* 1986;10(1):111-114.

28. McCann J, et al. Genital findings in prepubertal girls selected for nonabuse: a descriptive study. *Pediatrics.* 1990;86(3):428-439.

29. Muram D. Child sexual abuse—genital tract findings in prepubertal girls. I. The unaided medical examination. *Am J Obstet Gynecol.* 1989;160(2):328-333.

30. Dubowitz H, Black M, Harrington D. The diagnosis of child sexual abuse. *Am J Dis Child.* 1992;146(6):688-693.

31. Chadwick D. Community Organization of Services Needed to Deal with Child Abuse. In: Myers J, ed. *APSAC Handbook on Child Maltreatment.* Thousand Oaks, CA: Sage Publications; 1996.

32. Felitti VJ, et al. Relationship of childhood abuse and household dysfunction to many of the leading causes of death in adults. The Adverse Childhood Experiences (ACE) Study [see comments]. *Am J Prev Med.* 1998;14(4):245-258.

33. Herman JL. *Trauma and Recovery: The Aftermath of Violence— From Domestic Abuse to Political Terror.* New York, NY: Basic Books; 1997:7-14.

34. van der Kolk BA. The drug treatment of post-traumatic stress disorder. *J Affect Disord.* 1987; 13(2):203-213.

35. van der Kolk BA, et al. Disorders of Extreme Stress: The Empirical Foundation of a Complex Adaptation to Trauma. *J Trauma Stress.* 2005;18(5):389-399.

36. Cohen JA, et al. Psychosocial Interventions for Maltreated and Violence-Exposed Children. *J Soc Issues.* 2006;62(4):737-766.

37. Hechler D. *The Battle and the Backlash: The Child Sexual Abuse War.* Lexington, MA: Lexington Books; 1988.

Chapter 6

POLICIES AND POLITICS

This chapter will attempt to describe and explain developments in US public policy regarding child abuse, especially policies that affected the work of child abuse medical doctors.

Political processes in the US are not necessarily rational, but are driven by the attitudes and emotions of the electorate. Policymakers, in a democracy, must be exceedingly sensitive to these attitudes and emotions, or they do not remain in office.

Public attitudes about child abuse in the US generally include the irrational belief that the problem affects "somebody else." Additionally, there has always been a general attitude that the physical punishment of children, even children under a year of age, is acceptable. Professional groups, including social services, law enforcement, and justice workers, also shape public policy regarding child abuse.

DISCIPLINARY DEFINITIONS AND BOUNDARIES

As soon as child abuse was medically recognized in the 20th century, questions arose about who should deal with the problem and how. These questions remain unresolved at the time of this writing. Aside from being harmful to a child's physical and mental health, acts of abuse were often considered intolerable by social workers and, in many instances, violated existing laws. As a public awareness of child abuse dawned, social services for the poor also commenced, and social workers began to see child abuse in the impoverished families they visited.

Auguste Ambroise Tardieu[1] appears to have believed that child abuse was the jurisdiction of the criminal justice system, with forensic doctors contributing definitional and diagnostic support to legal authorities. When C. Henry Kempe and his associates rediscovered child physical abuse, they commenced psychiatric research to find the causes,[2] define risk factors, and provide preventative services.[3] They recognized that child abuse posed serious legal problems for the criminal justice system and for social workers obliged to stage coercive interventions in abusive homes.[4] Sociologists and social workers saw child abuse as a problem to which their knowledge and skills could be applied, although David Gil[5] proposed that poverty predisposed abuse. He suggested incidents of abuse would decrease as families' socioeconomic conditions stabilized. However, the reduction of poverty was a daunting political task that had been attempted in the 1960s by President Lyndon Johnson[6] (although not because of child abuse).

Johnson's Office for Economic Opportunity launched many programs to confront poverty, and the most successful was Head Start, which has provided early intervention as well as developmental enhancement services for children for a half-century. The program was first led by pediatrician Julius Richmond and later by psychologist Edward Zigler. There is strong evidence to suggest that the Head Start program improves parenting practices by teaching and by example and may prevent child abuse.[7,8]

Thus, 3 professional sectors claimed the problem of child abuse: criminal justice, social services, and health care. Social services would emerge as the dominant player, while the doctors in health care services diagnosed individual cases, employing personal, rather than public, health approaches. The public health sector remained uninvolved. State and local departments of public health generally did not undertake child abuse prevention. The involvement of the justice sector was limited to cases of abuse that constituted criminal acts and that could be prosecuted.

Kempe and his associates immediately recognized the need for local, multidisciplinary responses and began to build local child protection teams, representing all 3 professional sectors. Legal scholars such as F.V. Harper also recognized the need for more than one profession, or agency, to be involved in child abuse cases.[9,10]

THE POLITICAL CONTEXT

The first laws that addressed child abuse specifically were developed in the US in the 1960s and 1970s. It may be helpful to consider the social and political context of those times in order to understand who the laws affected and why.

Chapter 2 describes some of the 19th-century influences that led to the 20th-century improvements in the valuation of and concern for children. In the US, the famous case of Mary Ellen, which generated great publicity, launched public and private social services and gave impetus to the growth of the profession of social work. In the early 20th century, children began to receive some political attention, which grew out of grassroots concerns about child welfare. Dorothy Bradbury describes the history of the US Children's Bureau in *Four Decades of Action for Children: A Short History of the Children's*

Bureau.[11] The idea for this bureau was conceived around 1903 and was endorsed by President Theodore Roosevelt, who called it "a bully idea." His backing launched the idea, but it required legislation to provide the necessary resources. Nine years later, Congress passed the enabling legislation, and it was signed by President William Taft. Bradbury writes, "It received strong support from those struggling to protect dependent and neglected children. In its vanguard were the forces opposing child labor. Some of its vitality came from the fertile soil of the settlement house movement."[11]

Julia C. Lathrop was the first director of the Children's Bureau and was appointed by President Taft in 1912.[12] At that time, the law required that the director of the Bureau be appointed by the president and confirmed by the Senate. Currently, the director of the Children's Bureau is 3 levels removed from the Secretary of Health and Human Services. The Office of Child Abuse and Neglect is lodged in the Children's Bureau at a safe distance from centers of power.

In addition to child labor, the Children's Bureau immediately concerned itself with issues of maternal and child health (MCH), especially infant and maternal mortality. The development of "standards of care and protection" was high on Lathrop's agenda. In that era, the infant mortality rate was 124 first-year deaths per 1000 live births, while in 2004, it was 7 per 1000. The collection of such data was a new undertaking by the Children's Bureau and was unique in the world at that time.[11] It is now a standard metric for the international comparison of children's health and welfare.

The first US legislative effort to improve the health of mothers and infants was the Sheppard-Towner Maternity and Infancy Protection Act in 1921, which provided matching federal funds to states that established centers for the care of pregnant women and their infants. This legislation was (reflexively) opposed by organized medicine, because it provided federal funding for health care, and it was no longer funded after 1929. In 1935, Franklin Roosevelt's New Deal would revive it in Title V of the Social Security Act, which again provided grants to states for Maternal and Child Health Services and Services for Crippled Children. Title V persists to this day and in one state (Florida) is used to support medical evaluation and care for abused children.

THE CHILD ABUSE REPORTING LAWS

Kempe initiated the process that led to adoption of child abuse reporting laws. He was motivated by cases in which children with abusive injuries were released from hospitals or emergency departments and sent home only to return with more serious or fatal injuries. Kempe believed intervening and reporting these injuries to authorities could prevent further abuse.

Together with Katherine Bain and Katherine Oettinger of the US Children's Bureau, Kempe organized a meeting in Washington in May of 1962 to draft principles and model language for the child abuse reporting laws, which under the US Constitution, would need to be adopted by individual states. Kempe invited a number of like-minded professionals, including social worker Helen Boardman of Los Angeles and this author, a pediatrician who provided support to Boardman. In addition to doctors, Kempe invited lawyers, psychiatrists, and social workers, who contributed to the development of the principles and suggested language. The group produced a document,[13] which after some modification by attorneys, was adopted as federal policy and circulated to the states. All states passed child abuse reporting laws within the next 2 years.

When the child abuse reporting laws were adopted by the states, it was quickly decided that doctors of medicine should be mandated reporters, but other professionals involved with children, such as teachers, were also made mandated reporters after it became apparent that some of their pupils were victims of child abuse and neglect. Ultimately, almost all persons professionally involved with children would be named mandated reporters. Mandated reporters were insulated from retributive litigation by "immunity provisions."

Despite the consensus on *who* should report abuse, there was debate about whether reports should be made to law enforcement agencies, social service agencies, or even departments of public health. Most states eventually made law enforcement and public social services the mandated recipients of child abuse reports, and many states required that the 2 agencies share information from the reports.

THE CHILD ABUSE PREVENTION AND TREATMENT ACT

In the 1960s, each state passed a child abuse reporting law that designated mandated reporters as well as mandated recipients of reports of suspected child abuse. Recipients have the responsibility of investigating reports and then providing interventions appropriate to individual cases. Larger states, such as California and New York, further delegated these responsibilities to counties. The result was a jumble of policies and procedures with no national standard or uniformity of practice.

Richard Krugman[14] writes that this situation resulted in the development of the Child Abuse Prevention and Treatment Act of 1974 (CAPTA). This legislation was initiated by then-Senator Walter Mondale. At that time, there was national criticism of the programs for the poor that had been initiated by Johnson in the 1960s. As a result, Mondale was required to minimize the connection between poverty and child abuse and argue that persons from all social strata could be abusers of children. While this is true, it ignores the statistics that support Gil's argument linking poverty to an increased risk of abuse.

CAPTA required that state laws and regulations conform to national policies if the states were to receive federal subsidies for their child abuse programs, especially funds to pay for foster care. It also created a federal agency, the National Center for Child Abuse and Neglect (NCCAN), with funding to support discretionary research and development and demonstration programs that could be provided by academic and other nonprofit institutions plus a mandate to determine the incidence and prevalence of the abuse and neglect. NCCAN was lodged in the welfare component of the Department of Health Education and Welfare, renamed the Department of Health and Human Services in 1980. Because of these changes, NCCAN became a social service agency, rather than one concerned with public health. CAPTA's support of states favored child abuse services located in the departments of social services. Only Florida lodged some responsibility in its state department of children's medical services.

National Center for Child Abuse and Neglect
The first director of NCCAN was Douglas Besharov, an attorney appointed by President Richard Nixon and his Secretary of Health Education and Welfare, Caspar Weinberger. Besharov soon became deeply concerned with the proliferation of child abuse reports occurring in the late 1970s and early 1980s. He published a book describing how to recognize and report child abuse,[15] devoting much of it to the problem of "excessive reporting" and the high frequency of "unsubstantiated reports." He failed to recognize that in many states and counties, the term "unsubstantiated" actually meant "uninvestigated" and reflected the states' inability to investigate all the reports they received after the reporting laws took hold.

When it was first launched, NCCAN had substantial funding for discretionary granting to qualified applicants for research and development projects, but it was subsequently demoted from a "National Center" to an "Office," and its budget has been reduced to about $7 million per year, an insignificant amount.

Krugman[14] also describes the work of the National Advisory Committee on Child Abuse, authorized by the same legislation. The multidisciplinary committee was a group of the most knowledgeable and active experts working with child abuse and writing about it in the 1970s and 1980s. The group met over a period of about 8 years and generated 5 major reports, which were submitted to the 2 secretaries of Health and Human Services between August 1990 and April 1995. None of their suggestions were ever implemented at the federal level.

The Unique Florida Program

Florida is the only state to embed responsibility for child abuse in a department of children's medical services, a program unique to the state and designed by two pediatricians, Gerold Schiebler and Jay Whitworth. As the chair of the Department of Pediatrics at the University of Florida in Gainesville, Schiebler worked for years to build a productive relationship with the Florida legislature and the state executive branch in order to improve medical services to children. In this process, he became a very effective lobbyist at the state level and was able to enhance the political worth of children and the importance of the Children's Medical Services Division in the state Health and Human Services structure. He transformed a conventional and limited Crippled Children's Services Program into a broad-based support system that could assist children with a variety of health problems in receiving specialized care. The program used Federal Title V funding along with state funding.

By the early 1970s, Whitworth recognized that most children reported as "possibly abused" would be in need of comprehensive medical evaluation, and he established the first multidisciplinary, model children's crisis center in Jacksonville, Florida at the University Hospital. The center was staffed by child abuse pediatricians qualified to perform examinations that would determine whether or not abuse had occurred and, if it had, what methods of treatment were appropriate.

Schiebler and Whitworth succeeded in institutionalizing the child protection team model, first introduced by Kempe, using a combination of state, federal, and university funding and delivering services to thousands of abused children and their families. Within a few years, this model had been copied at 21 sites in the state of Florida, and currently, each of them maintains multidisciplinary team services for abused children. Unfortunately, this program has not been replicated in any other state.

DEVELOPMENTS IN CRIMINAL JUSTICE

The justice sector developed its own programs. The most important of these is a system of child advocacy centers (CAC).

CHILD ADVOCACY CENTERS

In the 1980s, Madison County Alabama District Attorney Robert E. Cramer established a safe and supportive system, originally known as "The Little House," for interviewing child sexual abuse victims in Huntsville, Alabama. This model made it possible for children to be skillfully interviewed in comfortable surroundings, in order to get the clearest possible descriptions of their abuse. The model quickly became popular with prosecutors.

Cramer was elected to Congress in 1990, and he succeeded in obtaining funding to launch CACs throughout the US based on the Huntsville model. In 2009, there were about 500 CACs in the US that have met the Huntsville standard. The Huntsville center itself became a national resource for child sexual abuse prosecution and victim support. Fewer than 20 CACs are based in hospitals; most are freestanding nonprofit agencies. The federal subsidy for each CAC is small, and most depend on state or local law enforcement resources as their main support.

ATTENTION TO VICTIMS OF CRIME

A scholarly field of "victimology" arose as a branch of criminology shortly after World War II. Victimology became a branch of US criminal justice practice in the late 1960s and 1970s when it was pointed out that more attention had been given to criminals than to their victims. At the federal level, the National Victim of Crimes Act (VOCA) was enacted in 1984, and most states provided services and support to identifiable crime victims, often contracting with hospitals or mental health providers for this purpose. David Finkelhor is a leader in establishing this field and published his book *Childhood Victimization* in 2008.[16] He expressed hope for a more significant public policy footprint for child maltreatment from the unifying concept of victims' importance.

FEDERAL SILOS

Federal initiatives for social services and justice work on child abuse grew substantially in the 1970s and 1980s; however, no comparable initiative for health work on child abuse has ever occurred. Although interdisciplinary and interagency child abuse work at the local level in counties and states is commonplace, such cooperation did not occur at the federal level and still does not. In the words of a retired US Surgeon-General: interagency cooperation at the federal level is considered "an unnatural act," resembling the mating of cats and dogs. Congress favors this view, because it allows members to cultivate pet projects (E. Brandt, personal communication, 1991). Better public policies concerning child maltreatment may require the development of a "public consciousness."

REFERENCES

1. Tardieu A. *Étude médico-légale sur les attentats aux mœurs.* Paris, FR: Librairie JB Baillière et Fils; 1857.

2. Steele BF, Pollock CB. A Psychiatric Study of Parents Who Abuse Infants and Small children. In: Helfer RE, Kempe CH, eds. *The Battered Child.* Chicago, IL: University of Chicago Press; 1968:103-145.

3. Gray JO, et al. Prediction and prevention of child abuse and neglect. *Child Abuse Negl.* 1977;1(1):45-58.

4. Helfer RE. The Responsibility and Role of the Physician. In: Helfer RE, Kempe CH, eds. *The Battered Child.* Chicago, IL: University of Chicago Press; 1968:43-58.

5. Gil DG. *Violence Against Children: Physical Child Abuse in the United States.* Cambridge, MA: Harvard University Press; 1973.

6. Johnson L. *The War on Poverty (Address to Congress).* Washington DC: Government Printing Office; 1965:375-380.

7. Parker FL, Piotrkowski CS, Peay L. Head Start as a social support for mothers: The psychological benefits of involvement. *Am J of Orthopsychiatry.* 1987;57(2):220-233.

8. Spieker S, et al. Enhancing Early Attachments in the Context of Early Head Start: Can Programs Emphasizing Family Support Improve Rates of Secure Infant-Mother Attachments in Low-Income Families? In: *Enhancing early attachments: Theory, research, intervention, and policy.* New York, NY: Guilford Press; 2005:250-275.

9. Harper FV. The Physician, The Battered Child and the Law. *Pediatrics.* 1963;31:899-902.

10. Bross DC, et al. *The New Child Protection Team Handbook.* 1988, New York, NY: Garland Publishing, Inc; 1988:624.

11. Bradbury DE. *Four Decades of Action for Children: A Short History of the Children's Bureau.* Washington, DC: US Government Printing Office; 1935.

12. Addams J, Scott AF. *My Friend, Julia Lathrop.* Champaign, IL: University of Illinois Press; 2004.

13. US Department of Health, EaW. *The Abused Child: Principles and suggested language for legislation on reporting of the physically abused child.* Washington DC: US Department of Health, Education, and Welfare; 1962.

14. Krugman RD. Child Protection Policy. In: Helfer ME, Kempe RS, Krugman RD, eds. *The Battered Child*. Chicago, IL: University of Chicago Press; 1997:627-641.

15. Besharov DJ. *Recognizing Child Abuse: A Guide for the Concerned*. New York, NY: Free Press; 1990.

16. Finkelhor D. *Childhood Victimization: Violence, Crime, and Abuse in the Lives of Young People*. New York, NY: Oxford University Press; 2008.

Chapter 7

HEALTH HARMS: HEALTH IMPAIRMENT RESULTING FROM ABUSE

The most significant damages produced by child maltreatment are health harms. While child abuse is an offense to justice and a debilitating social problem, its effects on the physical and mental health of individuals are the most costly. The maltreatment of infants and children produces significant damage to health with a wide variety of manifestations, including obvious physical damage and mental health effects that are often disabling. Many physical health harms have specific forensic implications. Neglect can result in significant physical harm and, in the case of infants, may be the direct cause of death. Because of accidents they may have while unsupervised, neglected toddlers are also at risk of fatality.

INJURY NOMENCLATURE AND CLASSIFICATION: AN HISTORICAL ANOMALY

During the era in which physical abuse was recognized and redefined by C. Henry Kempe, a problem of nomenclature arose in the injury field. Injury researchers, seeking pathways to injury prevention, began to reject the adjective "accidental," because it implied inevitability.[1] They divided injuries into 2 large classes, unintentional and intentional.

At about the same time, medical child abuse researchers, especially Kempe and Ray E. Helfer, were rejecting the adjective "intentional," because in most cases, it is difficult to determine the intent of the person responsible for the injuries. Instead, they invented the adjective "nonaccidental" to describe injuries inflicted by other persons and distinguishable from the common accidents of children. Child abuse reporting laws used the legal phrase "other than accidental," and the phrase "non-accidental trauma" was soon abbreviated by busy doctors to "NAT." This nosological problem still plagues researchers and practitioners, seeking to develop metrics to quantify child maltreatment and children's injuries.

FORENSICALLY IMPORTANT HARMS FROM ABUSE

As noted by Auguste Ambroise Tardieu and reemphasized by Kempe and others, certain medical conditions are pathognomonic for some types of abusive acts. Knowledge of these conditions is an important part of child abuse medicine.

TRAUMATIC BRAIN INJURY

In young infants past the early neonatal period, the most frequent cause of traumatic brain injury (TBI) (ie, mechanical damage to the brain) is shaken baby syndrome (SBS). Traumatic brain injury from abuse is also common in toddlers, but it is less specific in older children and adults in whom it may result from a variety of unintentional events, such as long falls and motor vehicle accidents. Because shaking[2] is a common practice of infant discipline, it is possible that mild or moderate TBI from shaking might be found in some children who lack histories of serious brain injury. There is currently no definitive diagnostic tool to identify children who suffer mild abusive brain injury.

The Shaken Baby Syndrome

In 1971, A. Norman Guthkelch[3] published case studies of infants with severe brain injury accompanied by subdural bleeding. The infants' caregivers had given histories of shaking just before changes in the infants' states of consciousness. Within a year or two, John Caffey[4] published on the same subject, and in 1974, he named the condition "whiplash shaken infant syndrome." Guthkelch and Caffey stressed that serious brain injury could be produced, without external head impact, by the violent shaking of infants. They also argued that the pathology specifically defined the injury mechanism. The specificity of the connection between pathology and injury mechanism has been challenged[5]; however, there is substantial consensus that the connection is valid. SBS has been included in the International Classification of Diseases (ICD) and is now recognized as a significant cause of infant mortality and morbidity.

BLINDNESS

Blindness is a frequent side effect of SBS. It may either be central as a result of occipital lobe brain damage or ocular as a result of direct damage to the eye or optic nerve. Typically, blindness occurs alongside TBI.

BONE INJURIES

As noted in *Chapter 3*, bone injuries were found to be a common result of physical abuse, but few of these injuries produce long-term or chronic disabilities. Many of them heal without treatment. The significance of bone injury in infants is its very high specificity for abusive injury. This connection was established empirically when children with bone injuries were sent home and then fatally injured.[6,7]

The Classic Metaphyseal Lesion

Paul K. Kleinman reviewed the classic metaphyseal lesion (CML) in 2008[6] and concluded that this bone lesion is highly specific for inflicted injury, although somewhat similar lesions may be observed in infants with rickets, extreme prematurity, and osteogenesis imperfecta. Pediatric radiologists can recognize and differentiate the metaphyseal lesion, but radiologists without pediatric experience often find it difficult.

Infants' Rib Fractures

According to Kleinman,[8] "Rib fractures in infants and young children are unusual, and any such injury should be regarded with suspicion. When causes such as prematurity, metabolic disorders, skeletal dysplasias and syndromes and motor vehicle and pedestrian accidents are excluded, most rib fractures in infants and young children are the result of abuse." They are sometimes discovered on chest x-rays that are taken on infants not known to have been injured, but are almost always indicators of serious physical abuse.

SKIN INJURY

Several types of skin injuries may result from abuse, including bruises, abrasions, lacerations, and burns. Of all these types, only burns are likely to produce long-term problems such as scarring or disfigurement. The patterns of skin injuries often reveal their abusive origins, reflecting the injuring object, eg, hand marks, lash marks, iron burns.

VISCERAL INJURY

The term "visceral" describes injuries to internal organs: lungs, heart, liver, spleen, kidneys, etc. Visceral injuries are often life threatening in the acute stage, but rarely produce long-term problems in survivors because the damaged organs (aside from the brain) can heal. They are caused by blunt mechanical force when children are stamped on or struck.

MUNCHAUSEN SYNDROME BY PROXY

The term "Munchausen syndrome by proxy" describes a type of abuse in which a caregiver fabricates or induces illness in his or her child, leading doctors to provide unnecessary—or even harmful—interventions as a result of the caregiver's false information.[9] In some cases, the caregiver actually produces the illness in the child by poisoning, suffocation, or other means. The eponym "Munchausen syndrome by proxy" is awkward and hard to explain; for that reason, Thomas A. Roesler and Carole Jenny have proposed the name of this condition be changed to "medical child abuse."[10]

Deprivational Failure to Thrive

"Failure to thrive" is a vague term that should be used only to describe the presenting situation of some infants with impaired growth or weight gain. Whenever possible, it should be replaced by more precise terms such as "undernutrition," "linear growth failure," or "developmental delay." Although "failure to thrive" is not a diagnosis, there are cases in which infants fail to gain weight and show signs of undernutrition that may be due to neglect by caregivers. This neglect can usually be proven by, first, ruling out specific medical disorders and then changing caregiver arrangements with resultant disappearance of the problem.

Mental Health and Developmental Problems

Since children are still growing, developmental aberrations are a major and unsurprising effect of child maltreatment. The aberrations tend to be more severe when the maltreatment occurs earlier in life. Lori Frasier[11] has pointed out the relationship between inflicted head injuries and developmental disabilities; however, since normal child development depends on nurture, the neglect of infants is also likely to interfere with normal cognitive, emotional, and social development.[12]

Developmental Disability

Neglect is a common cause of developmental delay.[13] The severity of the delay appears to be determined by the degree and duration of the neglect and by the age of the infant when neglect begins. Younger infants are more susceptible to the effects of neglect than older children. Developmental delay resulting from neglect is often reversible by good nurture.

Harms from Sexual Abuse

An early analysis by Ruth and C. Henry Kempe[14] suggested that harmful long-term effects were very common following sexual abuse, especially incest, and that boys were generally more affected by the abuse than girls. A more recent meta-analysis of extensive published literature confirms earlier observations, revealing significant emotional and mental problems resulting from sexual abuse.[15] Specific deleterious effects that are frequently observed include posttraumatic stress disorder (PTSD), depression, suicide, impaired academic performance, promiscuity, and the victim-perpetrator cycle.

POSTTRAUMATIC STRESS DISORDER

PTSD—a complex mental disorder involving reliving the traumatic event, depression, mood problems, and other symptoms—has been connected to sexual and physical abuse.[16-18] Effective therapies, employing cognitive behavioral techniques along with medications, are now widely available. Additionally, many mental health programs have been created to treat PTSD.

GENITAL INJURIES

Although many children with histories of sexual abuse do not have genital injuries, when such injuries are present, they may corroborate a history.[19] Many sexually abusive acts do not produce genital injuries. Genital injuries can also heal quickly, and a delay of days or weeks between the act and the exam can result in a false negative exam. Although many laypersons believe that a doctor can diagnose or exclude "virginity," this is often untrue.

SEXUALLY TRANSMITTED DISEASES

Sexually transmitted diseases (STD) may be indicators of sexual abuse[20]; however, many variables influence the specificity of this association. Newborns may acquire STDs during the birth process. When an STD is found, the examining physician must consider the child's age, the site of the infection, and the specific pathogen along with its biology.

MAJOR CHRONIC HEALTH PROBLEMS OF ADULTS

The connection of "adverse childhood experiences" to the long-term and life-limiting health problems of adults (such as cancer, heart disease, and stroke) has been established by multiple studies published by Vincent Felitti and his associates.[21-28] These associations are probably mediated by behaviors such as smoking, eating, and use of psychoactive substances. Based on observations from his own practice, Felitti estimates that about a third of the day-to-day work of internal medicine specialists is generated by child abuse via long-term unhealthy behaviors in survivors. Felitti's studies demonstrate the staggering financial and human costs of child maltreatment.

Current research suggests that improvements in childhood experiences and reductions in various forms of child maltreatment would result in a substantial reduction in health problems at all ages. Given that improvement in childhood experiences can be accomplished at a reasonable cost, programs that can produce such changes need to be extensively studied and developed (see *Chapter 12*). Felitti's work may succeed in bringing public health science to curtail the problem of child maltreatment.

GENERATIONAL EFFECTS OF ABUSE

PHYSICAL ABUSE

Having observed that many parents of physically abused children gave histories of having been abused themselves, Kempe and Brandt Steele[29] pointed out the likelihood of generational transmission of the propensity for physical child abuse. This observation stimulated studies that indicated only about a third of abused children later abused their own children.[30] Two theories were advanced to explain this data. One theory suggested that biologically-based resilience allowed some children to escape long-term deleterious effects of abuse.[31] Another theory held that some form of "rescue" had occurred in the form of support by an adult. The child's relationship with the "rescuer" supplanted the earlier abusive relationship. Both theories are plausible and not mutually incompatible.

INTER-GENERATIONAL TRANSMISSION OF INCEST

The occurrence of incestuous sexual abuse spanning more than 2 generations in a family has been described repeatedly,[32] and this occurrence is commonplace. Since many, if not most, human behaviors are learned in a family setting, it is hardly surprising. A genetic basis for pedophilia has been proposed, but is not established.[33]

OTHER CRIMINAL BEHAVIORS

In a number of studies, Cathy Spatz Widom[34-37] has demonstrated that abused children are at risk for an increased incidence of criminal behaviors when they become adults, but such outcomes are by no means inevitable and are strongly influenced by intervening variables. The harms to health caused by child abuse warrant its inclusion as a major threat to the public health and give child abuse prevention a high priority.

Health problems resulting from child maltreatment are a major public health problem, perhaps the most important public health problem that can be specifically identified. Certainly, it is now evident that, in the US, a major public health effort is needed to prevent child maltreatment or (to put it more positively) to improve the childhood experience. While recent efforts by the Centers for Disease Control are steps in the right direction, much greater resources are needed and could be utilized effectively as knowledge of child maltreatment prevention continues to grow. In addition, public health professionals at the state and local levels need to become more involved in child maltreatment prevention.

REFERENCES

1. Committee on Trauma Research, Institute of Medicine US. *Injury in America: A Continuing Public Health Problem.* Washington DC: National Academies Press; 1985.

2. Theodore AD, et al. Epidemiologic features of the physical and sexual maltreatment of children in the Carolinas. *Pediatrics.* 2005; 115(3):e331-337.

3. Guthkelch AN. Infantile subdural hematoma and its relationship to whiplash injuries. *Br Med J.* 1971;2:430-431.

4. Caffey J. On the theory and practice of shaking infants. Its potential residual effects of permanent brain damage and mental retardation. *Am J Dis Child.* 1972;124(2):161-169.

5. Uscinski RH, McBride DK. The shaken baby syndrome: an odyssey. II Origins and further hypotheses. *Neurol Med Chir (Tokyo).* 2008;48(4):151-155; discussion 155-156.

6. Kleinman, PK. Problems in the diagnosis of metaphyseal fractures. *Pediatr Radiol.* 2008;38(suppl 3):S388-394.

7. Kleinman PK. Multiple fractures in the long bones of infants suffering from chronic subdural hematoma—a commentary. *AJR Am J Roentgenol.* 2006;187(6):1403-1404.

8. Kleinman P. Bony Thoracic Trauma. In: Kleinman, PK, ed. *Diagnostic Imaging of Child Abuse.* St. Louis, MO: Mosby; 1998.

9. Meadow R. Munchausen syndrome by proxy. The hinterland of child abuse. *Lancet.* 1977;2(8033):343-345.

10. Roesler TA, Jenny C. *Medical Child Abuse.* Elk Grove Village, IL: American Academy of Pediatrics; 2008.

11. Frasier LD. Abusive head trauma in infants and young children: a unique contributor to developmental disabilities. *Pediatr Clin North Am.* 2008;55(6):1269-1285, vii.

12. Johnson DE. Adoption and the effect on children's development. *Early Hum Dev.* 2002;68(1):39-54.

13. Hildyard KL, Wolfe DA. Child neglect: developmental issues and outcomes. *Child Abuse Negl.* 2002;26(6-7):679-695.

14. Kempe R, Kempe CH. *The Common Secret: Sexual Abuse of Children and Adolescents.* New York, NY: W.H. Freeman & Company; 1984.

15. Paolucci EO, Genuis ML, Violato C. A meta-analysis of the published research on the effects of child sexual abuse. *J Psychol.* 2001;135(1):17-36.

16. Herman JL. *Trauma and Recovery: The Aftermath of Violence—From Domestic Abuse to Political Terror.* New York, NY: Basic Books; 1997:7-14.

17. Ackerman PT, et al. Prevalence of post traumatic stress disorder and other psychiatric diagnoses in three groups of abused children (sexual, physical, and both). *Child Abuse Negl.* 1998;22(8):759-774.

18. Herman JL, Harvey MR. Adult memories of childhood trauma: a naturalistic clinical study. *J Trauma Stress.* 1997;10(4):557-571.

19. Christian CW, et al. Forensic evidence findings in prepubertal victims of sexual assault. *Pediatrics.* 2000;106(1 Pt 1):100-104.

20. Bays J, Chadwick D. Medical diagnosis of the sexually abused child. *Child Abuse Negl.* 1993;17(1):91-110.

21. Felitti VJ. Long-term medical consequences of incest, rape, and molestation. *South Med J.* 1991;84(3):328-331.

22. Felitti VJ. Childhood sexual abuse, depression, and family dysfunction in adult obese patients: a case control study. *South Med J.* 1993;86(7):732-736.

23. Felitti VJ. [The relationship of adverse childhood experiences to adult health: Turning gold into lead]. *Z Psychosom Med Psychother.* 2002;48(4):359-369.

24. Felitti VJ, et al. Relationship of childhood abuse and household dysfunction to many of the leading causes of death in adults. The Adverse Childhood Experiences (ACE) Study [see comments]. *Am J Prev Med.* 1998;14(4):245-258.

25. Hillis SD, et al. The association between adverse childhood experiences and adolescent pregnancy, long-term psychosocial consequences, and fetal death. *Pediatrics.* 2004;113(2):320-327.

26. Hillis SD, et al. Adverse childhood experiences and sexually transmitted diseases in men and women: a retrospective study. *Pediatrics.* 2000;106(1):E11.

27. Brown DW, et al. Re: asthma and the risk of lung cancer. Findings from the Adverse Childhood Experiences (ACE). *Cancer Causes Control.* 2006;17(3):349-350.

28. Chapman DP, et al. Adverse childhood experiences and the risk of depressive disorders in adulthood. *J Affect Disord.* 2004;82(2):217-225.

29. Steele BF, Pollock CB. A Psychiatric Study of Parents Who Abuse Infants and Small Children. In: Helfer RE, Kempe CH, Eds. *The Battered Child.* Chicago, IL: University of Chicago Press; 1968:103-145.

30. Kaufman J, Zigler E. Do abused children become abusive parents? *Am J Orthopsychiatry.* 1987;57(2):186-192.

31. Anthony EJ, Cohler BJ. *The Invulnerable Child.* New York, NY: Guilford Press; 1987.

32. Cooper I, Cormier BM. Inter-generational transmission of incest. *Can J Psychiatry.* 1982;27(3):231-235.

33. Quinsey VL. The etiology of anomalous sexual preferences in men. *Ann NY Acad Sci.* 2003;989:105-17, 144-153.

34. Widom CS, Schuck AM, White HR. An examination of pathways from childhood victimization to violence: the role of early aggression and problematic alcohol use. *Violence Vict.* 2006;21(6):675-690.

35. Widom CS, Weiler BL, Cottler LB. Childhood victimization and drug abuse: a comparison of prospective and retrospective findings. *J Consult Clin Psychol.* 1999;67(6):867-880.

36. Widom CS, et al. Long-term effects of child abuse and neglect on alcohol use and excessive drinking in middle adulthood. *J Stud Alcohol Drugs.* 2007;68(3):317-326.

37. Widom CS, Ames MA. Criminal consequences of childhood sexual victimization. *Child Abuse Negl.* 1994;18(4):303-318.

Chapter 8

FORENSIC MEDICAL EVIDENCE OF MALTREATMENT: SECURING JUSTICE, DETERRING CRIME, JUSTIFYING COERCIVE INTERVENTION

Forensic medical work occupies a substantial amount of child abuse doctors' time. This chapter explains the interactions between medical science and the legal system, as these 2 sectors approach the problem of child maltreatment.

ADVERSARIAL LEGAL PROCESSES

The origins and nature of the adversarial legal process are closely tied to the development of democracy[1] but are beyond the scope of this book. Many different legal systems exist, but the US and most other English-speaking countries use the adversarial legal process. In the adversarial process, opposing attorneys, representing the defendant and plaintiff, compete to convince a judge and jury of the defendant's guilt or innocence. The attorneys build a case for—or against—the defendant by presenting their best analyses of the case with supporting evidence. The jury later renders a verdict, which the judge may uphold or overturn. A fair trial must precede any restriction of adult citizens' democratic civil liberties, including the right to care for and raise children in accordance with personal beliefs, unless those beliefs are obviously harmful.

THE NEED FOR DOCTORS AS WITNESSES

Soon after child abuse reporting laws were enacted, many doctors soon learned that simply reporting a child's injury as "other than accidental" and leaving further investigation and intervention to "authorities" might be a prescription for a catastrophic outcome. Often, the only tangible sign of abuse is the medical evidence of "battering," or inflicted injury. If the child's caregivers maintain a clean, organized household and persistently declare their innocence, authorities may see no reason to remove the child from their care, leaving the child susceptible to further abuse. Medically-discovered child abuse is analogous to a potentially fatal disease, such as meningitis; if it is properly diagnosed and treatment administered, a positive outcome can be achieved. But if the diagnosis is missed or the intervention inadequate, the outcome could be fatal.

Learning experiences of this sort led pediatrician Ray Helfer[2] to urge doctors to participate in legal processes, whether they be criminal prosecutions of abusive caregivers or legal actions taken to remove children from abusive environments. Helfer expressed doubt that criminal prosecutions stopped future abuse, but encouraged doctors to contribute their expertise anyway, hoping that most cases would be resolved using civil, rather than criminal, proceedings. Often, when doctors participated, the legal outcome led to better protection of abused children. With the medical expertise to qualify injuries as "not accidental," doctors perceived an ethical obligation to bear witness. Still, most doctors found the process of litigation unfamiliar, and many physicians were deterred from becoming involved in child abuse cases because of this discomfort.

THE DOWNSIDE: ADVERSARIAL DISTORTION

In an adversarial trial, each side is represented by a lawyer, whose task it is to examine and present evidence. Lawyers reconstruct crimes by questioning 2 types of witnesses: fact witnesses and expert witnesses. Fact, or percipient, witnesses testify to the facts of the case as they know them. Expert witnesses employ specialized knowledge and experience to interpret facts. For example, in a case concerning child abuse, a medical doctor may use his or her expertise to explain the likely mechanisms of certain types of injuries. Medical doctors may testify in either capacity. The selective suppression, emphasis, or distortion of the information presented to the jury is the business of trial attorneys; thus, any trial can become a test of the facts and their interpretation as well as the persuasive capabilities of the contending lawyers. When presenting "admissible evidence," trial lawyers are not limited by legal or ethical considerations. Admissibility is the only test, and admissibility is a complex, rule-bound legal concept that is often significantly affected by lawyers' capabilities.

Irresponsible Expert Witnesses

All witnesses take a legal oath, promising to uphold the truth. In the case of expert witnesses, who interpret facts, the truth may be distorted or omitted, making the oath ineffective. Irresponsible expert witnesses are frequently encountered in cases involving child abuse and other medical issues. Irresponsible testimony takes a number of forms, including going outside of the witness' experience, propounding unique theories, altering case facts, and outright lying.[3,4] Judges have used case law to improve the reliability of expert witnesses, but the problem of irresponsible testimony persists.[5]

Compensation

In litigated child abuse cases, rates of $450 per hour are not unusual, especially for defense witnesses. Rates for prosecution witnesses are usually limited by the budgets of public institutions. Compensation for expert testimony may be 4 to 5 times greater than doctors' usual compensation in other types of practice, and 8 to 10 times greater than that of academic psychologists and other scientists.

Litigation-Generated Science and Publication: Controversy Creation

Expert witnesses may enhance their value by publishing articles that support the points they wish to make in court. While an argument has been made that litigation-generated science is the same as any other,[6] the legal arena is a poor place to settle scientific disagreements. The purpose of litigation is always to win, but the purpose of science is to know.

Many published articles about various types of child abuse are litigation generated. A remarkable example is furnished by Dr. Jerold Lucey, the editor of the prestigious journal *Pediatrics*, who accepted an article describing the familial (and possibly genetic) occurrence of sudden infant death syndrome (SIDS), only to learn years later that 2 of the cases described had been successfully prosecuted as homicides and were not the result of SIDS.[7]

SPECIFIC ISSUES IN CHILD ABUSE FORENSIC MEDICINE AND SCIENCE

A number of specific issues have surfaced repeatedly in litigated child abuse cases. Among them are the following:

— The accuracy and veracity of children's statements about their abuse histories

— The methods by which children's histories are taken by professional interviewers

— The likelihood that the interviewer might influence the content of children's statements

— The nature and validity of memory

— The effects of various forms of child abuse and the damages that might occur and that should be assessed against abusers

— The effects of minor injury events common in childhood, as they might or might not produce severe damage—more specifically, the likelihood of serious injury resulting from short falls

— The possible effects produced by shaking

— The specificity of certain types of bony injury for abuse

— The physical findings of genital injury associated with child sexual abuse

— The specificity of the occurrence of sexually transmitted diseases in young children

— The likelihood that certain diseases mimic the medical findings of child abuse

ILLUSTRATIVE CASES

All of the following cases **(Table 8-1)** were high profile in the sense that they received significant public attention, and each of them illustrates a way in which distortion of truth can be a product of the adversarial process. Some examples of litigation-driven publications about child abuse issues are displayed in the following table.

PHYSICAL ABUSE CASES

The detailed review of individual cases provides insight into the distortions that can occur during litigation.

Table 8-1. Litigation-Driven Publications About Child Abuse Issues.

ISSUE	AUTHOR	REFERENCE
The accuracy and veracity of children's statements about their abuse histories	**Wakefield**	*Accusations of Child Sexual Abuse*[7]
The nature and validity of memory	**Lombardi**	*New York*[8]
The likelihood of death or serious injury resulting from short falls	**Loftus**	*American Psychologist*[9]
The possible effects produced by shaking	**Ommaya**	*British Journal of Neurosurgery*[10]
The specificity of certain types of bone injury for abuse	**Plunkett**	*The American Journal of Forensic Medicine and Pathology*[11]
Child abuse diagnosis requires "absolute certainty"	**Keller and Barnes** **Loftus**	*Pediatric Radiology*[12] *American Psychologist*[9]

LISA STEINBERG AND JOEL STEINBERG

The case of Elizabeth "Lisa" Steinberg came to light in a 911 call to the New York City dispatcher early on the morning of November 2, 1987. The responding police officers and paramedics found a 6-year-old child covered with bruises, unconscious, and not breathing in the care of her adoptive parents Joel Steinberg and Hedda Nussbaum. Nussbaum also appeared bruised.

Born to a 19-year-old college student, Lisa was adopted by Steinberg, a lawyer who sometimes arranged adoptions, but who, in this case, completely eschewed adoption proceedings, simply taking the newborn baby home to his partner, Nussbaum. Steinberg repeatedly battered Nussbaum and later began to abuse the child as well. Neighbors were aware of the abuse and made reports to law enforcement and Child Protective Services. Although both cases were investigated, no interventions took place. In that era, interventions for battered women who did not prosecute their assailants were still infrequent. Interventions for battered children, however, were customary.

Both adults stated that Lisa had been unconscious for hours before the call was made to 911. Nussbaum said her fear of Steinberg kept her from calling sooner.

At the hospital, Lisa was declared brain dead, and life support was discontinued. An autopsy was performed by the medical examiner for the city of New York, and the medical findings, noted prior to and after death, supported a diagnosis of battered child syndrome. Lisa had multiple skin injuries of differing ages to all parts of the body and a head injury, the apparent result of several blows to the head.

In the opinion of the experts who testified for the prosecution, the blows were forceful and beyond the capacity of the frail and injured Nussbaum, who was in the home with Lisa, Steinberg, and another younger child; thus, Steinberg was identified as the perpetrator.

The prosecutor made no charges against Nussbaum. Steinberg was convicted of first-degree manslaughter. The jury deliberated for 8 days and spent much of this time questioning Nussbaum's innocence. Nussbaum watched the child die and didn't call for help, although Steinberg had left the house and did not prevent her from calling. Nussbaum's testimony helped convict Steinberg, while defense attorney Barry Scheck's sympathetic portrayal of Nussbaum helped her escape conviction.

The trial was the first in the US to be televised and grossed high ratings. Steinberg was released from prison in 2004, after serving 16 years.[13]

THE CAMBRIDGE *AU PAIR* CASE: MATTHEW EAPPEN

On February 4, 1997, Louise Woodward, the *au pair* hired by physicians Sunil and Deborah Eappen to care for their infant son, Matthew, frantically called police to report the boy was having trouble breathing. Matthew's parents were at work at the time Woodward made the call. Four days later, Matthew died as a result of severe brain swelling accompanied by subdural bleeding and retinal hemorrhages. Child abuse doctor Eli Newberger and the clinicians who cared for Matthew found the injuries resulted from shaken baby syndrome and reported their suspicion of nonaccidental injury.

The Massachusetts Medical Examiner performed an autopsy and concluded the death was due to a head injury, most likely resulting from impact against a firm surface. The death was classified a homicide, and following investigation, the district attorney brought charges of homicide against Woodward.

Woodward had been recruited by EF Education Inc., a commercial provider of *au pair* services. EF Education Inc. recruited famed criminal defense attorney Barry Scheck to defend her. Scheck made his foray into child abuse when he defended Hedda Nussbaum, the battered partner of Joel Steinberg.

A major part of Scheck's strategy was to put the parents on trial in place of Woodward. In order to do so, he needed to create doubt about the timing of the injury, planting the suspicion that one of the parents had injured the infant. Scheck argued that a child could receive a fatal head injury, but still appear well for hours or days before suddenly collapsing. Chicago neuropathologist Dr. Jan Leestma reinforced Scheck's claim, testifying that the bleeding in Matthew's head was a few weeks old, and his death had resulted from rebleeding in an old subdural hematoma, a novel theory at the time of the Eappen case. Systematic studies of this issue had not been published in early 1997, but subsequent studies of children with fatal head injuries, where the exact time of injury is known, have shown the scenario presented by Woodward's defense is unlikely.[14,15]

The jury convicted Woodward of second-degree murder, but the judge converted the conviction to involuntary manslaughter and released her. This case illustrates the effectiveness of diverting judicial attention to persons other than the defendant. The judge became convinced of Woodward's lack of intent and overruled the jury.

CHRISTOPHER AND HARRY CLARK (REGINA V. SALLY CLARK)

This case took place in the United Kingdom and involves the sudden and unexpected deaths, in 1996 and 1999, of 2 infants born to the same mother in succession. Byard[16] has reviewed most of the medical information in the case; however, the original trial (in 1999) and appeal transcripts are available and the case has been subjected to multiple appeals and analyses. In the United Kingdom, it received extensive media coverage as well as extraordinary public scrutiny, and it resulted in the public denunciation of 2 of England's most respected child abuse doctors.[17]

According to Byard:

"On 13 December 1996, Christopher Clark, at the age of 11 weeks, was found dead by his mother. Following an autopsy, the cause of death was initially recorded as lower respiratory infection, but this was changed to suffocation following a review of the findings after his 8-week-old brother, Harry, had subsequently been found dead by his mother on 26 January 1998.

"The initial reported autopsy findings for Christopher included minor laceration and bruising of the frenulum of the upper lip, recent intra-alveolar hemorrhage, hemosiderin-containing macrophages in the lungs, and multiple small bruises of the limbs. His only significant clinical history was of a bleeding nose two weeks before death in a London hotel room where his family was staying. His father had been looking after him at the time and hotel staff had witnessed the episode.

"Harry's initial reported autopsy findings included a healing fracture of the right second rib, costochondral fracture-dislocation of the right first rib, retinal haemorrhages, retinal hemosiderin deposition and inflammation, acute inflammation and bruising of the paraspinal muscles, extradural haemorrhage and swelling of the spinal cord, cerebral hypoxia–ischaemia, cerebral laceration and hemorrhage, occasional petechial haemorrhages of the left eyelid, hemorrhage on the surface of the eyeballs, and hemosiderin staining of the meninges. Death was initially attributed to shaken-impact syndrome, which was then revoked in favour of a diagnosis of inflicted suffocation."

Unfortunately, there was no photographic documentation of the gross anatomical findings. Another error was that postmortem cultures of the infant Harry that grew staphylococcus were not reported or discussed in the medical examiner's report, and this oversight was later interpreted as an attempt at concealment of a possible diagnosis of infection as a cause of death. Most experienced pathologists place little credence in the importance of postmortem cultures because they are so often contaminated; however, in this case, Byard[16] accepts them as possibly indicative of a real infection contributing to death.

Dr. Timothy David was an instructed expert for the defense of Sally Clark. He offered an opinion that the blood in the lungs of Christopher could be accounted for by primary pulmonary hemosiderosis, a rare but natural condition. Although both parents had been near the infants around the time of their being found dead, both were found dead by the mother, and the father might have had an alibi for the time of Harry's death; therefore, only Sally Clark was indicted and tried for their homicide. She was convicted and sentenced to prison, where she served 2 years before her conviction was overturned on appeal.

Despite the fact that neither infant met the definition of SIDS, the prosecutor emphasized the rarity of SIDS in back-to-back siblings. Professor Sir Roy Meadow testified about the possibilities of suffocation, and he was asked about the probabilities of SIDS occurring in 2 successive infants. He cited a statistical probability of about one in 83 million births, using a recently published governmental report on sudden unexpected death in infants.[18] This was not an appropriate use of the SIDS statistics; however, it was irrelevant, since SIDS can be firmly excluded in both cases.

Based on a complaint made by Sally Clark's father, Meadow was censured by the General Medical Council (GMC), the governmental organization that licenses medical doctors in the United Kingdom. Meadow was stricken from the register of licensed physicians because a consultant for the GMC believed he had given bad testimony, but later appealed that decision successfully.[17]

Another event that occurred during the Clark case involved another child abuse doctor, David Southall, who added another opinion. The issue of the nosebleed in Christopher's case had not been publicized, and Southall learned of it after Sally Clark was convicted and sent to prison. Since the only person on the scene at the time of the nosebleed was the father and not the mother, Southall offered testimony to the effect that the father was likely responsible for the suffocation. At that point in the case, a third infant born to the same couple was being considered for placement with the father, which caused Southall to become concerned for that infant's safety.

In a bizarre turn of events, the protective service authorities asked Southall to meet with David, who was consulting for them about the case of the third baby. David was conflicted because he had been retained by Sally Clark for her defense in the criminal case. He was also a permanent consultant for the GMC. Subsequently, Southall was stricken from the register by the GMC for offering testimony in the case. The exact reasons for this action are unclear.

The Clark case has had a chilling effect on child abuse medicine in the United Kingdom. Some pediatricians no longer accept assignments in which they may be required to provide opinions about abused children.[19] The GMC has lost credibility as a competent licensing agency capable of judging the work of doctors, especially in the complex area of child protection.[17] While serious errors were made by the pathologist who performed the autopsies on both infants, the testimony provided by Meadow and Southall was competent and responsible.

PHILLIP BUELL AND KENNETH MARSH

In the early afternoon of April 27, 1983, a telephone call came to Dr. Irvin Kaufman at the Children's Hospital in San Diego, requesting transport and ongoing care for an injured 2-year-old boy who was in an emergency room at a nearby hospital and in severe distress, apparently as a result of a very recent head injury. In the emergency room, he was posturing and intermittently apneic. The boy, Phillip Buell, was supported with assisted ventilation via an endotracheal tube and given fluid resuscitation. At Children's Hospital he was discovered to be brain dead, and a report of the case was made to the coroner. The autopsy demonstrated that he had died as a result of a severe head injury with an impact site on the left side of his head. Phillip also had some recent bruises on his shoulder and back as well as 3 gashes on the back of his neck.

His past medical history included a hospitalization 3 months earlier for intra-abdominal bleeding due to unexplained abdominal trauma accompanied by bruising on both the abdomen and the back. The bruising was carefully documented in a sketch by the ICU nurse. In addition, he had unexplained fractures of the first metacarpal bones of both hands with differing dates of injury, and he had had a facial injury with a torn labial frenulum and 3 or 4 additional prior episodes of poorly explained bruising.

An investigation of the scene where the head injury had taken place was made. Following a review of the medical information and the scene investigation, the case was prosecuted, and Kenneth Marsh, the mother's partner and the man who was with Phillip at the time of his fatal head injury, was convicted of second-degree murder. Marsh was sentenced to 15 years to life in the California State Prison, and the verdict was unsuccessfully appealed.

Twelve years later, in 1995, a petition for a writ of habeas corpus was filed on behalf of Marsh. The petition cited new evidence, but it was actually based upon new interpretations of the old evidence by 2 new medical experts. The experts were Dr. Paul Wolfe, a pathologist at the local San Diego Veterans Administration Hospital who had no pediatric experience, and Dr. Khalil Jiraki, who was a medical examiner in Michigan. Wolfe and Jiraki argued that Buell had a pre-existing coagulopathy and bled into his head as a result of minor trauma. The petition was opposed by the district attorney of San Diego County and was dismissed by a judge.

Seven years later, lawyers associated with the California Innocence Project filed a new petition for a writ of habeas corpus. Once again Marsh's defense claimed that there was new evidence supporting the theory of the pre-existing coagulopathy. There was no new evidence, but there were new experts that reviewed previously introduced evidence. The new experts included Drs. Michael Innes of Australia and Gregory Reiber of Sacramento; later on, Drs. Thomas Schweller, John Plunkett, Janice Ophoven, and Jan Leestma joined the endeavor.

By this time, Marsh had served about 18 years in state prison and the newly elected district attorney of San Diego County, Bonnie Dumanis, decided not to oppose the petition. Marsh's 1983 conviction was set aside, and he was released from prison. Shortly afterward, he filed a claim against the State of California for false imprisonment and was awarded damages in the amount of $720 000. He then sued the county of San Diego, Children's Hospital, and the doctors who had been involved in diagnosing Phillip's case as one of child abuse, asking for $50 million. The suit alleged that the doctors and the prosecutor had conspired to deprive Marsh of his right to a fair trial by falsifying the medical facts of the case.

On May 6, 2009, a federal judge dismissed Marsh's suit, basing the order on a lack of evidence supporting any of the allegations and on the immunity provisions of the California child abuse reporting law. The suit had been mostly based on the same allegations as the petition for a writ of habeas corpus, which was unopposed by the San Diego district attorney and resulted in the early release of Marsh from prison as well as the setting aside of the 1983 guilty verdict.

Given this finding, this author offers the opinion that the case of Phillip Buell and Kenneth Marsh was one of "innocence manufactured" by the California Innocence Project assisted by irresponsible expert witnesses. It went as far as it did because the elected district attorney of San Diego County mistakenly accepted Marsh's 2002 petition despite the absence of evidence to support it.

SEXUAL ABUSE CASES

In the 19th century most persons assumed that child abuse was rare or nonexistent. In the 20th century more people were prepared to believe it might occur, but in the particular case of sexual abuse, disbelief was more particularly pervasive. The legal system had its own intrinsic prejudices.

SYSTEMIC JUDICIAL PREJUDICE

Australian judge Jocelynne Scutt traces the origins of prejudice against women and girls who complain of rape to the work of Matthew Hale, a 17th-century legal scholar[20] who famously said,

"The husband cannot be guilty of a rape committed by himself upon his lawful wife, for by their mutual matrimonial consent and contract, the wife hath given herself in kind unto the husband which she cannot retract." Hale is also known for saying, "Rape is an accusation easily to be made, hard to be proved, and harder yet to be defended by the party accused, tho' never so innocent." Sigmund Freud's 19th-century theory of fantasy amplified and fortified this latter view.

She makes the point that precedent and prejudice on this issue are embedded firmly in the English Common Law and its descendents in the English-speaking countries and that judges are often prejudiced against female witnesses of any age. Substantial work by 19th-, 20th-, and 21st-century feminists may be reducing the prejudice. Feminist philosophy of law refers to a body of scholarship that has grown out of and is closely associated with the feminist reform movement that began in the mid-20th century. It is concerned with analyzing legal structures, with identifying their effects on the material condition of women and girls, and with formulating new structures or reforms that could correct gender injustice, exploitation, or restriction. Thus, it is the critique of law as a patriarchal institution.

Child sexual abuse cases have always been difficult to prove in court, but cases involving children who are very young or who are handicapped by developmental disability or other communication problems, such as deafness, remain especially difficult. It is possible that such children are more often targeted as sexual objects by adults simply because they may not be able to provide credible testimony about their abuse.

Despite these obvious difficulties, in the early 1980s, cases of child sexual abuse involving young children in childcare settings began to be reported and prosecuted. More cases of abuse were reported, partly because of a rapid increase in the use of childcare services following the poverty programs of the 1960s. Widespread public and professional attention to the problem led David Finkelhor to publish a book about it in 1988 based on a national survey.[21]

THE MCMARTIN CASE

The McMartin case involved the parents of young children attending a childcare center who reported their suspicions of abuse, which led to an investigation.

The preliminary hearing and trial of the case took place between 1987 and 1990. It set records for the number of charges, complexity of evidence, and time duration and costs of the trial. David Hechler's book, *The Battle and the Backlash*, was published in the midst of this struggle in 1988. In proper journalistic style, Hechler interviewed many of the principal persons involved in McMartin, but he was limited by legal constraints at the time. His book provides in-depth analyses of many other cases for which the legal processes were already complete.

Hechler makes it abundantly clear that he was a "war correspondent," and the war produced numerous battles. There were more than 2 sides since conflicting viewpoints on a number of important issues were being argued at the time. The usual adversarial conflicts between prosecutors and defense attorneys were complicated by additional disagreements among investigators in law enforcement agencies, social workers in Child Protective Services, children's therapists and interviewers, and, in some cases, child abuse doctors. Methods of interviewing children were still undergoing testing, and the significance of various anatomical findings were still being debated.

However, the most significant issue was the two-centuries-old denial of the reality of child sexual abuse, and although the defendants of the McMartin case were acquitted and many skirmishes were lost, that particular issue was put to rest. Child sexual abuse was finally recognized as a real issue.

KILLING THE MESSENGER

McMartin and other cases in that era shed light on another phenomenon that has subsequently been employed frequently by criminal defense attorneys and others who wish to make child abuse legal cases disappear. This method involves focusing intense criticism on professional persons who provide support to children and testify on behalf of children. In the McMartin case, the targets included Kee MacFarlane, who conducted most of the children's interviews, the child abuse doctors Astrid Heger and Bruce Woodling, and the psychiatrist Roland Summit. The attacks most often took place in the mass media, but they also occurred in litigation-generated professional publication, as in this example from Lee Coleman writing in the *IPT* journal,[22]

"Based on my own viewing of videotapes of 46 children in the McMartin case, I can state categorically that the children were in every single session outrageously manipulated by their interviewers. During the past five years, I have studied about 700 hours of audio- or videotapes in cases of alleged child sexual abuse. All too many show a pattern of interviewing techniques aimed at getting a child to admit abuse rather than to find out if any has occurred."

Denial of reality and messenger-killing are also used in cases of physical abuse, and especially in cases of Munchausen syndrome by proxy and suffocation.

CONCLUSION: FIXING THE PROBLEMS

A legal system that works quite well for many sorts of disputes has frequently failed in dealing with child abuse cases. Its repair may require an engineer who has not yet appeared on the scene. It is certainly beyond the scope of this book. Until major changes occur, child abuse doctors will need to be wary, but still will not be able to avoid involvement in litigation.

REFERENCES

1. Kagan RA. *Adversarial Legalism: The American Way of Law.* Cambridge, MA: Harvard University Press; 2003.

2. Helfer RE. The Responsibility and Role of the Physician. In: Helfer RE, Kempe CH, eds. *The Battered Child.* Chicago, IL: University of Chicago Press; 1968:43-58.

3. Brent RL. The irresponsible expert witness: a failure of biomedical graduate education and professional accountability. *Pediatrics.* 1982;70(5):754-762.

4. Chadwick DL, Krous HF. Irresponsible expert testimony by medical experts in cases involving the physical abuse and neglect of children. *Child Maltreat.* 1997;2:315-321.

5. Satiani B. Expert witness testimony: rules of engagement. *Vasc Endovascular Surg.* 2006;40(3):223-227.

6. Boden LI, Ozonoff D. Litigation-generated science: why should we care? *Environ Health Perspect.* 2008;116(1):117-122.

7. Wakefield H, Underwager R. *Accusations of Child Sexual Abuse.* Springfield, IL: C.C. Thomas; 1988.

8. Lombardi J. Defending Joel Steinberg. New York Web site. http://nymag.com/nymetro/news/people/features/9607. Published May 21, 2005. Accessed June 21, 2010.

9. Loftus EF. The reality of repressed memories. *Am Psychol.* 1993;48(5):518-537.

10. Ommaya AK, Goldsmith W, Thibault L. Biomechanics and neuropathology of adult and paediatric head injury. *Br J Neurosurg.* 2002;16(3):220-242.

11. Plunkett J. Shaken baby syndrome and the death of Matthew Eappen: a forensic pathologist's response. *Am J Forensic Med Pathol.* 1999;20(1):17-21.

12. Keller KA, Barnes PD. Rickets vs. abuse: a national and international epidemic. *Pediatr Radiol.* 2008;38(11):1210-1216.

13. Hobbs CJ. Skull fracture and the diagnosis of abuse. *Arch Dis Child.* 1984. 59(3):246-252.

14. Starling SP, et al. Analysis of perpetrator admissions to inflicted traumatic brain injury in children. *Arch Pediatr Adolesc Med.* 2004;158(5):454-458.

15. Willman KY, et al. Restricting the time of injury in fatal inflicted head injuries. *Child Abuse Negl.* 1997;21(10):929-940.

16. Byard RW. Unexpected infant death: lessons from the Sally Clark case. *Med J Aust.* 2004;181(1):52-54.

17. Chadwick DL, Krous HF, Runyan DK. Meadow, Southall, and the General Medical Council of the United Kingdom. *Pediatrics.* 2006;117(6):2247-2251.

18. Fleming P, et al, eds. *Sudden Unexpected Deaths in Infancy.* London, Eng: The Stationery Office; 2000:159.

19. Williams C. United Kingdom General Medical Council fails child protection. *Pediatrics.* 2007;119(4):800-802.

20. Scutt JA. Confronting Precedent and Prejudice: Child Sexual Abuse in the Courts. In: Oates RK, ed. *Understanding and Managing Child Sexual Abuse.* Sydney, Australia: W.B. Saunders; 1990.

21. Finkelhor D, Williams LM, Burns N. *Nursery crimes: sexual abuse in day care.* Los Angeles, CA: Sage Publications; 1988.

22. Coleman L. Learning From the McMartin Hoax. Institute for Psychological Therapies Web site. http://www.ipt-forensics.com/journal/volume1/j1_2_7.htm. Published in 1989. Accessed June 21, 2010.

Chapter 9

RESISTANCE, DENIAL, INDIFFERENCE, AND BACKLASH

Though it be honest, it is never good
To bring bad news; give to a gracious message
A host of tongues, but let ill tidings tell
Themselves when they be felt.

— **William Shakespeare**, from *Antony and Cleopatra*

Child abuse is bad news, and information about it is unwelcome. As a result, medical doctors who have described abuse have met with a variety of negative reactions, including overt opposition, indifference, denial, and backlash.

OVERT OPPOSITION, DENIAL, AND BACKLASH

C. Henry Kempe, a pediatrician who crusaded for early identification and treatment of child abuse, once received an anonymous death threat,[1] and according to his wife and collaborator, Ruth Kempe, he also received criticisms from other pediatricians, who charged him with dramatizing the problem of child abuse.[2] Doctors, who treated battered infants before the publication of Kempe's seminal 1962 article "The Battered Child Syndrome," feared going public with their diagnoses of abuse.[3]

Sigmund Freud was isolated by his Viennese peers for attributing "hysteria" to child sexual abuse. He wrote to his friend, German otolaryngologist Wilhelm Fliess,[4] "I am as isolated as you could wish me to be. The word has been given out to abandon me, and a void is forming around me." Faced with professional ruin, Freud devised a new theory that his patients' allegations of abuse were fantasies. Psychiatrist Roland Summit was bitterly attacked for his description of child sexual abuse accommodation syndrome, a theory that sought to explain the compliance of sexually abused children,[5] when his observations were used in litigation of criminal child abuse cases.

Roy Meadow and David Southall, 2 British pediatricians who proved that parents sometimes intentionally suffocate their infants, were stricken from the register of licensed doctors by the General Medical Council, the United Kingdom's statutory medical licensing agency.[6] Southall's use of covert video surveillance in the hospital was singled out for attack, even though it saved children's lives by proving their caregivers were asphyxiating them.[7]

French child psychiatrist Catherine Bonnet reported a case of child sexual abuse, and her medical license was revoked when the child's father complained.[8] Despite the immunity provisions of reporting laws, child abuse doctors in the US are sometimes sued for reporting child abuse cases.

INDIFFERENCE

In the 19th century, Auguste Ambroise Tardieu convincingly described the pathology of child abuse.[9] There is no recorded contradiction of his work, but none of his colleagues or successors expanded on it.

In the 1980s, a medical school's faculty committee told Jill Glick[10] (with painful honesty) that working on child abuse was "an academic dead end." Almost all child abuse medical research done before the year 2000 was accomplished without federal support, and child abuse is still not a priority for the National Institutes of Health.

In 1999, Frank Putnam, a well-published researcher who studies abuse and its effects, left the National Institute of Mental Health to work for a private foundation that offered more support for his work. For the most part, the health care research establishment, consisting of the National Institutes of Health, the Centers for Disease Control, and the medical schools, has been indifferent to the problem of child abuse and has provided little support for doctors who pursue solutions to medical problems connected to child maltreatment. In this author's view, this indifference (by "good men") has retarded progress in the child abuse field more than active opposition.

There are many gaps in medical knowledge about child abuse, but governmental support for medical research is paltry,[11] despite the obvious health harms abuse causes.[12] Denial of obvious and confirmed observations may serve political purposes, as in the case of wars of choice; economic purposes, as in the case of smoking hazards[13]; or avoidance of costly remedies, as in the case of AIDS.[14] There is a need for better understanding of our society's avoidant behavior with respect to child abuse; however, it is clear that doctors who study and report child abuse cannot expect to be welcomed in medical circles or other arenas.

This chapter will attempt to describe those aspects of resistance and denial that are obvious and can be documented as well as institutional abuse and the various organizations that suffer from it. An explanatory theory might incorporate ideas from this chapter.

THE HUMAN SELF-IMAGE: COMING TO GRIPS WITH REALITY

The human capacity for self-deception is strong and can block accurate perceptions of reality. For example, Charles Darwin's theory of evolution challenges the human self-image and, therefore, has generated enormous resistance despite being supported by scientific data. It is hard to accept demotion from a god-like being with dominion over all animals to the status of just one more biological entity, subject to the same rules and principles as all other living things.

The observation that parents and caregivers can sometimes violently and volitionally harm their infants and children presents a similar challenge for the human self-image. The difficulties in acceptance may be reduced if the people who abuse children can be categorized as "different" from most of society. Linking child abuse to poverty or mental disorder may facilitate professional and public acceptance. Eliminating the poverty linkage, as Walter Mondale set out to do in 1974 (see *Chapter 6*), may have been politically unwise.

FRAMING THE WORLD IMAGE

With funding from Prevent Child Abuse America (PCAA) and other foundations, a research organization called Frame Works Institute developed a publication titled "Reframing Child Abuse" and released it on the PCAA Web site.[15] Developed with the use of focus groups, "Reframing Child Abuse" advances the theory that the American public sees child abuse as an issue from which they are removed, something done by and happening to someone else. Abuse is not seen as a part of a continuum, involving general social mores about authority in families, physical punishment, or sexual behavior. "Reframing Child Abuse" posits that effective prevention requires a major change in public attitudes and proposes more sophisticated marketing approaches by organizations, such as PCAA.

Concern about the public image of child abuse may have motivated Vincent Felitti to use the alternate term "adverse childhood experience" to describe the abusive events in early life that predispose to later illness in adults.[12] By substituting the more neutral term, he increased the chances that his work would be accepted for publication by a public health journal. If this approach continues to be successful, a change of language for child abuse prevention should be considered. Perhaps "preventing child abuse" should be replaced with "improving the childhood experience."

THE CRIMINAL JUSTICE LINKAGE

Defining child abuse as a crime automatically made it the subject of adversarial argument. Law enforcement officers and prosecutors tended to favor this approach. Some doctors, and, most notably, Ray Helfer questioned it. Defendants and their advocates opposed it, both on a case-by-case basis and as a policy. Vigorous opposition became backlash. Doctors who testified in criminal cases were singled out for criticism.

ORGANIZED RESISTANCE BY PERPETRATORS
Persons suspected of child abuse naturally seek to avoid punishment. They argue that they are falsely accused and may band together to demonstrate that false accusations are common. This resistance contributes to the problem of denial. Perpetrators may argue that child sexual abuse exists only in the minds of zealots, does not constitute abuse or criminal activity, and should be tolerated by society.

The North American Man-Boy Love Association
The North American Man-Boy Love Association (NAMBLA) is an organization whose members favor the decriminalization of sexual activity between men and boys. On its Web site,[16] NAMBLA quotes major literary figures Walt Whitman, Oscar Wilde, and Allen Ginsberg. Ginsberg specifically supported NAMBLA. The writings of Wilde and Whitman seem to support the group's doctrine. The organization advocates eliminating the concept of an age of consent (for both genders) and argues for the benefits of sex between adults and children. Most of their arguments were answered by David Finkelhor[17] in 1979; however, NAMBLA still appears to be a functioning advocacy group.

The Guyon Society
In contrast, the defunct Guyon Society, a pro-pedophilia organization based in Los Angeles, had a short lifespan. The group's members were attracted to the writings of former French justice René Guyon, who had published a book on the ethics of sex.[18] Though often compared to NAMBLA, the Society held to Guyon's tenets, which required mutual consent between sexual partners, and spokespersons for the group repeatedly asserted that its members did not violate laws protecting children from sexual abuse.

Victims of Child Abuse Laws
Members of Victims of Child Abuse Laws (VOCAL) characterize themselves as victims of inappropriate criminal prosecution or coercive social interventions aimed at protecting their children. They band together to resist these actions and attack persons and agencies that engage in child protection. VOCAL has an active and well-developed Web site[19] as well as many state chapters.

The False Memory Syndrome Foundation
False memory syndrome (FMS), a term coined in 1992 by the False Memory Syndrome Foundation (FMSF), describes the group's theory

that adults, who belatedly remember instances of childhood sexual abuse, may be mistaken about the accuracy of the recalled events. A defense of persons prosecuted for child sexual abuse, the syndrome has not been recognized for inclusion in the *Diagnostic and Statistical Manual of Mental Disorders* (DSM-IV and DSM-V) or in the International Classification of Diseases (ICD-CM)—the formal nomenclatures of medical and psychological conditions. The FMSF has a well-developed Web site[20] and publishes a newsletter. Its board of directors consists of persons accused of prior abuse by their grown children and academics, who are also expert witnesses in many litigated cases.

The Innocence Project

Created by Barry Scheck, a famous New York criminal defense attorney, the Innocence Project uses DNA technology to exonerate persons who may have been convicted of crimes based on older evidence, such as witness statements. Though the Innocence Project does not generally handle child physical abuse cases, except rapes in which DNA evidence might play a part, California's version of the Project took up the case of Kenneth Marsh, a man incarcerated for the second-degree murder of his girlfriend's 2-year-old son. Because there was no evidence to support anything but the conviction that had taken place in Marsh's 1983 trial, the California Innocence Project had to manufacture his innocence from scratch. The effort succeeded because San Diego County's newly elected district attorney, Bonnie Dumamis, decided not to oppose the petition for habeas corpus that resulted in Marsh's release, and he was freed from prison after serving 21 years of a 25-year sentence. Marsh was subsequently paid about $750 000 in damages by the state.

INSTITUTIONAL CHILD ABUSE AND INSTITUTIONAL RESISTANCE TO REMEDIATION

The term "institutional child abuse" is used to describe maltreatment occurring in institutions, such as churches, schools, or extracurricular organizations. Such cases differ substantially from those that occur in the community or in private homes. Institutions have their own special instincts for survival, and when illegal or intolerable things occur within them, the institutions tend to protect themselves in any way they can. When a teacher, priest, coach, or volunteer scoutmaster abuses a child, the parent institution often attempts to reduce its liability by effecting a transfer, temporary suspension, or some other palliative action, rather than seeking a more permanent remedy. This behavior, though understandable, often allows the institutionalization of the abuse itself. Thus, institutions may impede rational understanding of child abuse.

CHILDCARE

A substantial growth in the use of childcare occurred in the 1970s, following the poverty programs of the 1960s. Increased use of daycare coincided with the rediscovery of child sexual abuse by social workers and other professionals, and the relationship between the two was undeniable. Still, it was associated with substantial public attention and resulted in a special survey by Finkelhor.[21] Many cases were closely scrutinized, and one resulted in a full-length book.[22]

Physical abuse cases also occurred in daycare settings; however, they did not occur in large, licensed daycare centers, but were confined mostly to situations in which a single caregiver supervised large groups of infants or small children. In contrast to "family daycare," large, licensed daycare centers appear to have a protective function for serious and fatal injuries,[23] whether abusive or accidental.

SCHOOLS

All forms of child abuse have been reported to occur in schools, including emotional,[24] physical, and sexual abuse.[25] In addition, abuse often comes to light in school settings, and teachers are mandated reporters of child abuse in all states in the US. Tolerance for corporal punishment in schools appears to be declining.[26] While some authorities equate corporal punishment with physical abuse,[27] that definition is not yet widely accepted.

RELIGIOUS INSTITUTIONS

Religious institutions play a variety of roles in child abuse. While Christian doctrines value children and call for them to be treated with kindness, Biblical writings (particularly the Old Testament Book of Proverbs) are also cited in support of harsh physical punishment. Instances of incest can also be found, though not condoned, in the Bible. Most organized religions encourage the participation of children, who are placed under the supervision of religious mentors, who may abuse them. Religious beliefs are also used to justify medical neglect with catastrophic consequences in some cases.[28]

The Catholic Church

In 1992, investigative reporter Jason Berry published a book describing the pervasive and enduring sexual abuse of children by Catholic priests.[29] Berry's book also documented tolerance of the abusive behaviors by authority figures within the Church's hierarchy. His observations have been confirmed by Patrick J. Wall, a former Roman Catholic priest who now works as an attorney specializing in clergy sexual abuse,[30] and many other qualified observers both inside and outside the Church.

The following passage is a good description of the problem of clergy sexual abuse. John Allen, a writer, cites Father Tom Doyle who states,[31]

"The clergy sexual abuse nightmare is far from simple and certainly far from ended. The bishops repeat the same empty mantra: they have norms in place from Dallas, 2002 and these have taken care of the problem. Perhaps from their limited bureaucratic viewpoint that particular blank on the page has been filled, but it has had a minimal effect on their awareness of the depth of harm done or pain caused not simply by the actual sexual abuse but by the often cold, distant and seemingly uncaring attitude of the hierarchy. True, many bishops and many more priests have responded heroically and compassion-ately, but the majority are frozen in a block of clericalist denial."

The Catholic Church has used intimidation to silence child victim-witnesses and their families in litigated court cases, threatening excommunication for persons who seek redress against the Church.[29] The Catholic Church has contributed to the problem of resistance to a rational description of child abuse.

Other Churches and Religions
Child sexual abuse has been reported in other churches and religious denominations.[32] It would be astonishing if it did not occur in almost all of them, and an accurate comparison of sects would be very difficult to carry out.

YOUTH SERVICE ORGANIZATIONS
Because adolescents have some autonomy and may sometimes exercise it, their abuse and exploitation has a different dynamic than the maltreatment of younger children. Still, the abuse of adolescents and young adults is a problem requiring attention.

The Boy Scouts of America
In the 1980s, a number of child sexual abuse cases were reported, concerning the Boy Scouts of America. The attendant adverse publicity and civil lawsuits led the organization to develop a sophisticated prevention program.[33] The prevention program is an optional part of training for new leaders but has never been rigorously evaluated. Unlike the Catholic Church, the Boy Scouts organization openly recognized its problem and addressed it forthrightly.

Boys and Girls Clubs of America
With problems similar to those of the Boy Scouts of America, the Boys and Girls Clubs of America (BCGA) have also developed formal and sophisticated prevention programs. In recent years, these programs have shifted their emphasis to the prevention of online youth exploitation.

DOCTORS, HOSPITALS, AND MENTAL HEALTH PROVIDERS

The medical literature about abuse perpetrated in health care settings, including psychiatric settings, is sparse. Feldman has conducted a survey that suggests this subject should have more study.[34] Quadrio studied 8 cases of abuse by therapists and suggested that they were inadequately investigated.[35] Although this sort of self-analysis is difficult and painful, much more research in this area is needed.

BETTER PREVENTION, THEORY, AND FRAMING ARE NEEDED

There is a clear need to reframe child abuse for the public in order to gain the political weight required to deal with the problem in a long-lasting and effective way. However, the major forms of child maltreatment are so different from each other as to constitute virtually separate problems with very different preventive approaches. Although they have in common a disregard for children's needs and rights, it is unlikely that all forms of abuse will fit into a single frame.

A theory to explain societal denial of child abuse must take into account multiple motives, including human self-image, perpetrator resistance, costs of control, institutional self-preservation, sacred doctrine, and shame.

Developmental psychologist Erik Erikson provides an eloquent description of the problem and the need for a unified stance, condemning abuse[36]:

"Someday, maybe, there will exist a well-informed, well considered and yet fervent public conviction that the most deadly of all possible sins is the mutilation of a child's spirit; for such mutilation undercuts the life principle of trust, without which every human act, may it feel ever so good and seem ever so right is prone to perversion by destructive forms of conscientiousness."

REFERENCES

1. Kempe A. *A Good Knight for Children: C. Henry Tempe's Quest to Protect the Abused Child.* Booklocker; 2007.

2. Kempe RS. *Personal Communication.* 2003.

3. Silverman FN. Letter/Commentary. *Pediatr Radiol.* 1994;24: 541-542.

4. Masson JM. *The Assault on Truth: Freud's Suppression of the Seduction Theory.* New York, NY: Ballantine Books; 2003.

5. Olafson E, Corwin DL, Summit RC. Modern history of child sexual abuse awareness: cycles of discovery and suppression. *Child Abuse Negl.* 1993;17(1):7-24.

6. Chadwick DL, Krous HF, Runyan DK. Meadow, Southall, and the General Medical Council of the United Kingdom. *Pediatrics*. 2006;117(6):2247-2251.

7. David TJ. Spying on mothers [letter; comment]. *Lancet*. 1994; 344(8915):133.

8. Bonnet C. *Personal Communication*. 2008.

9. Labbe J. Ambroise Tardieu: the man and his work on child maltreatment a century before Kempe. *Child Abuse Negl*. 2005;29(4):311-324.

10. Glick JC. *Personal Communication*. 2009.

11. Krugman RD, Leventhal JM. Confronting child abuse and neglect and overcoming gaze aversion: the unmet challenge of centuries of medical practice. *Child Abuse Negl*. 2005;29(4): 307-309.

12. Felitti VJ, et al. Relationship of childhood abuse and household dysfunction to many of the leading causes of death in adults. The Adverse Childhood Experiences (ACE) Study [see comments]. *Am J Prev Med*. 1998;14(4):245-258.

13. Carter SM, Chapman S. Smoking, disease, and obdurate denial: the Australian tobacco industry in the 1980s. *Tob Control*. 2003;12 Suppl 3:iii23-30.

14. Ben-Zur H, et al. Denial of HIV/AIDS and preventive behaviour among Israeli adolescents. *J Adolesc*. 2000;23(2):157-174.

15. Prevent Child Abuse America. *Reframing Child Abuse and Neglect for Increased Understanding and Engagement*. http://www.preventchildabuse.org/about_us/reframing/ documents.shtml. Accessed July 14, 2010.

16. NAMBLA. http://www.nambla.org. Accessed July 14, 2010.

17. Finkelhor D. What's wrong with sex between adults and children? Ethics and the problem of sexual abuse. *Am J Orthopsychiatry*. 1979;49(4):692-697.

18. Guyon R. *Sex Life & Sex Ethics*. London, Eng: John Lane; 1933.

19. VOCAL. http://www.vocalofmo.org/. Accessed July 14, 2010.

20. False Memory Syndrome Foundation. http:// www.fmsf online.org/about.html. Accessed July 14, 2010.

21. Finkelhor D, Williams LM, Burns N. *Nursery crimes: sexual abuse in day care*. Los Angeles, CA: Sage Publications; 1988.

22. Hollingsworth J. *Unspeakable Acts: The True Story of One Community's Nightmare*. New York, NY: Contemporary Books; 1986.

23. Chadwick D, Phillips M. Safety in Numbers: Protecting Children From Death and Serious Injury by Licensed Childcare Centers. In: Alexander R, ed. *Child Fatality Review: An Interdisciplinary Guide and Photographic Reference*. St. Louis, MO: G.W. Medical Publishing, Inc.;709-713.

24. Krugman RD, Krugman MK. Emotional abuse in the classroom. The pediatrician's role in diagnosis and treatment. *Am J Dis Child.* 1984;138(3):284-286.

25. Miller T. SESAME. http:// www.sesamenet.org. Accessed July 14, 2010.

26. American Academy of Pediatrics. Committee on School Health. Corporal punishment in schools. *Pediatrics.* 2000;106(2 Pt 1): 343.

27. Straus MA, Donnely DA. *Beating the Devil Out of Them: Corporal Punishment in American Families*. San Francisco, CA: Lexington Books; 1994.

28. Asser SM, Swan R. Child fatalities from religion-motivated medical neglect. *Pediatrics.* 1998;101(4 Pt 1):625-629.

29. Berry J. *Lead us not into temptation: Catholic priests and the sexual abuse of children.* Champaign, IL: University of Illinois Press; 1992.

30. Wall P. Patrick J. Wall. http://patrickjwall.wordpress.com/. Accessed July 14, 2010.

31. Allen JL. Fr. Tom Doyle on 'Crimen Sollicitationis.' National Catholic Reporter Web site. http://hcronline.org/node/4530. Published October 13, 2006. Accessed July 14, 2010.

32. Taylor C, Fontes, LA. *Seventh Day Adventists and sexual child abuse.* In *Sexual abuse in nine North American cultures: Treatment and prevention.* Sage Publications, Inc: Thousand Oaks, CA; 1995:176-199.

33. Potts LF. The youth protection program of the Boy Scouts of America. *Child Abuse Negl.* 1992;16(3):441-445.

34. Feldman KW, Mason C, Shugerman RP. Accusations that hospital staff have abused pediatric patients. *Child Abuse Negl.* 2001;25(12):1555-1569.

35. Quadrio C. Sexual abuse involving therapists, clergy and judiciary: Closed ranks, collusions and conspiracies of silence. *Psychiatry, Psychol and Law.* 1994;1(2):189-198.

36. Erikson E. *Young man Luther: a study in psychoanalysis and history.* 2nd ed. New York, NY: W.W. Norton & Company; 1993.

Chapter 10

Treatment for Child Abuse

Healing is a matter of time, but it is sometimes also a matter of opportunity.

— **Hippocrates**

Child abuse, in its various forms, causes conditions often amenable to treatments that speed recovery. This chapter will briefly describe some conditions and treatments known at present.

A General Requirement: Stop Ongoing Abuse

Although it may seem obvious, a general requirement for treating the physical, mental, and emotional health harms produced by child abuse is to stop ongoing abuse. Therapists seeing children with mental health problems may not be aware of ongoing abuse, but must always be alert to the possibility. In some cases of child abuse or neglect, it is sufficient to interrupt the maltreatment and provide good general supportive nurturing care in a family setting.

Treatment of Physical Injuries

Treatment of physical injuries resulting from abuse is similar to treatment of injuries that are incurred unintentionally and is described in textbooks.[1] Unlike unintentional injuries, injuries specific to child abuse may require special forensic studies. For example, when examining a child with a head injury, it may be necessary to examine the retina more than once during the early hours and days of care. In some cases, a magnetic resonance imaging (MRI) of the head may be needed for forensic purposes, whereas a computed tomography (CT) scan would suffice for the guidance of care.

A variety of injuries result from physical abuse. These include bruising, burns, head injuries, and skeletal injuries of varying degrees of severity. Injuries to the internal organs, including the abdominal viscera, heart, and lungs may also result from physical abuse. In some studies, it appears that abusive injuries are more severe than accidental ones and have a higher fatality rate. This is probably an artificial effect related to definitions.

TREATMENT OF MENTAL AND DEVELOPMENTAL PROBLEMS

All forms of child abuse often result in mental and/or developmental problems, but the specific effects of abuse types are not predictable.[2-7] A majority of maltreated infants and children taken into the care of social agencies have identifiable mental health or developmental problems in need of remediation.[8]

TREATMENT FOR DEVELOPMENTAL PROBLEMS

Problems in cognitive, emotional, and social development are prevalent in children who have been neglected or abused. The younger the child the greater the likelihood that he or she will struggle with developmental problems.[9,10] These problems may differ from those due to nonabusive traumatic experiences. There is abundant evidence that enhanced childcare programs can prevent and treat developmental problems.[11]

Programs must provide both emotional and cognitive nurture to infants and young children and must be intensive, high quality, and ecologically pervasive in that they enable parents to provide ongoing support and stimulation after professional helpers are no longer present. Decades of longitudinal research at the University of North Carolina, Frank Porter Graham Center document major, persistent effects of early intervention for at-risk infants and children who might otherwise experience a variety of ill-effects.

Child abuse medical centers need to include services of this sort in population-accessible sites. School districts make good partners for these programs, because personnel with the skills to accommodate special needs are often employed as instructors.[12]

THE FAMILY CONTEXT

Infants, toddlers, and school-aged children require support from adults or older children and are greatly helped by larger family groups or even "villages." They thrive when surrounded by widening circles of affection. Mental health care must include the child's supportive family member(s).

TREATMENT SETTINGS AND ORGANIZATION

Treatments for abused children and adults need to be organized around the conditions and needs that are encountered in a given population. It is efficient to connect treatment programs to diagnostic and documentation services provided in child abuse medical centers, since many of the children seen for diagnosis need care. Many different forms of mental health care may be needed, and the types of care tend to change with advances in research.

Remediation should be tailored to the individual, and clinical assessments and standardized tests can help to determine the appropriate type of treatment. Most of the children in a given population can be treated on an ambulatory basis while remaining in their homes or foster homes. Some children require residential care, often for social, rather than therapeutic, reasons, but sometimes for both. Residential and shelter programs for abused children often provide mental health services on-site.

All infants and children, taken into out-of-home care for protective reasons, should be promptly evaluated for mental health and developmental status.[13] After evaluation, they should be provided with mental health care and/or developmental enhancement programs suited to their needs.

TREATMENT MODALITIES

There are literally hundreds of treatment modalities for various mental health problems. Most modalities, in current use, fall into the general category of cognitive behavioral therapy (CBT).[14] Medication is also often used along with therapy.[14] Psychiatrists, psychologists, and social workers are educated about the details of treatment modalities. Pediatricians at child abuse medical centers should familiarize themselves with the current popular methods of care.[15]

ACCESS TO CARE

Serious physical abuse resulting in life-threatening injury is rare, and one trauma center can serve a population of a few million. Conversely, mental health problems resulting from abuse or neglect are prevalent as are children in need of skilled interviewers and medical examiners, and mental health care services are usually provided on an ambulatory basis, with weekly visits spanning several months. Decentralization of clinics and offices is necessary to alleviate the strain placed on health care providers and make therapy accessible to as many people as possible.

A national survey of child welfare service directors, at the county level,[16] supports the value of "evidence-based therapy," but does not provide explicit guidance useful to program providers in this field.

CHILD ABUSE DOCTORS' ROLES

Only pediatrics has established criteria for a subspecialty in child abuse. Most child abuse medical centers are directed by child abuse doctors, who are also pediatricians. Some centers offer the services of psychiatrists experienced in child abuse, but most will not until more psychiatrists become trained in the treatment of abused children. At present, training requirements for psychiatric residents include competency in the recognition of abused persons, but there is no standard for competently treating abused children. In practice, most of the mental health and developmental care provided to abused children and their family members comes from providers who are not physicians. Arrangements for supervision and quality control vary depending on local conditions and require systematic, objective measurement.[15]

A Trauma Assessment Pathway Model

Using the most current information available, the Chadwick Center for Children & Families in San Diego (with support from the National Child Traumatic Stress Network) has developed an assessment framework for understanding traumatized children and making informed clinical decisions regarding these children.[17] The *Assessment-Based Treatment for Traumatized Children: A Trauma Assessment Pathway* (TAP) uses a multifaceted assessment process to enable clinicians to gain an in-depth understanding of the child; his or her developmental level and traumatic experience; and the family, community, and cultural system in which he or she lives. This information is used to effectively triage and treat the child and family as well as assist the clinician in making decisions throughout the treatment process.[15] Standardized mental health status instruments such as the Trauma Symptom Checklist for Children are employed before, during, and after treatment in order to provide objective measurements of change.

In recent years, researchers have contributed to major improvement of mental health care.[14,18-32] These contributions have led to the development of what are now considered to be the best practices, and these evolve rapidly.

QUALITY, COSTS, AND BENEFITS OF CARE

Given the prevalence of child abuse and its deleterious effects on health, there is a continuing need for therapeutic services until such time as prevention programs become effective and the prevalence of abuse is reduced. The cost of care is an issue, and costs must be weighed against benefits.

In recent years, several methods of mental health care, assuring favorable cost-benefits ratios and a high number of positive outcomes, have emerged. The TAP model described previously is one way of achieving a sound assessment and holistic care. Peer review ensures that the type of care provided is recognized and accepted by a community of therapists. The peer review community should involve more than one institution and one locality in order to provide a balance of viewpoints.

CONTINUOUS QUALITY IMPROVEMENT (CQI)

Continuous Quality Improvement (CQI) describes a set of principles developed in manufacturing industries and recently adapted to health care by Donald Berwick, president of the Institute for Healthcare Improvement, and others.[33,34] Some of the principles include

— Accurate and complete descriptions of processes, including process variations

— Carefully defined desirable outcomes and methods for their measurement

— Ongoing emphasis on reduction of process variability

— Statistical methods for defining the relationships of process variation to outcome

— Reduction of emphasis on individual practitioner errors

— Emphasis on innovation by practitioners

Assessment-based therapy, as described by Robyn Igelman[15] adapts easily to CQI as outlined above. Assessment-based therapy as described allows for comparison of the effectiveness of a number of treatment variables including therapists, specific treatment details, and comparison over time. This makes CQI possible.

All children identified as having been abused can and should be provided with competent mental health care to reduce long-term deleterious effects. Competent care must include documentation of healing.

REFERENCES

1. Fuhrman BP, Zimmerman JJ, eds. *Pediatric Critical Care.* St. Louis, MO: Mosby; 1997.

2. Bifulco A, et al. Exploring psychological abuse in childhood: II. Association with other abuse and adult clinical depression. *Bulletin of the Menninger Clinic.* 2002;66(3):241-258.

3. Brown J, et al. Childhood abuse and neglect: Specificity and effects on adolescent and young adult depression and suicidality. *J Am Acad Child Adolesc Psychiatry.* 1999;38(12): 1490-1496.

4. Cole CB. The specificity of long-term effects of sexual abuse and factors mediating outcome: A comparison of sexually and physically abused young adults. In: *Dissertation Abstracts International.* Ann Arbor, MI: ProQuest Information & Learning; 1988:2373-2373.

5. Fonagy P, et al. Attachment, the reflective self and borderline states: The predictive specificity of the Adult Attachment Interview and pathological emotional development. In: *Attachment theory: Social, developmental, and clinical perspectives.* Hillsdale, NJ: Analytic Press, Inc.; 1995:233-278.

6. Gibb BE, Chelminski I, Zimmerman M. Childhood emotional, physical, and sexual abuse, and diagnoses of depressive and anxiety disorders in adult psychiatric outpatients. *Depression Anxiety.* 2007;24(4):256-263.

7. Orbach Y, et al. The effect of being a victim or witness of family violence on the retrieval of autobiographical memories. *Child Abuse Negl.* 2001;25(11):1427-1437.

8. Leslie LK, et al. The physical, developmental, and mental health needs of young children in child welfare by initial placement type. *J Dev Behav Pediatr.* 2005;26(3):177-185.

9. Nelson CA III, et al. The effects of early deprivation on brain-behavioral development: The Bucharest Early Intervention Project. In: *Adolescent psychopathology and the developing brain: Integrating brain and prevention science.* New York, NY: Oxford University Press; 2007:197-215.

10. Ramey CT, Farran DC, Campbell FA. Predicting IQ from mother-infant interactions. *Child Dev.* 1979;50(3):804-814.

11. Ramey CT, Ramey SL. Early intervention and early experience. *Am Psychol.* 1998;53(2):109-120.

12. McCormick MC, et al. Early intervention in low birth weight premature infants: results at 18 years of age for the Infant Health and Development Program. *Pediatrics.* 2006;117(3): 771-780.

13. Leslie LK, et al. Addressing the developmental and mental health needs of young children in foster care. *J Dev Behav Pediatr.* 2005;26(2):140-151.

14. Cohen JA, Berliner L, Mannarino AP. Psychosocial and pharmacological interventions for child crime victims. *J Trauma Stress.* 2003;16(2):175-186.

15. Igelman R, et al. Creating More Trauma-Informed Services for Children Using Assessment-Focused Tools. *Child Welfare.* 2007;86(5):15-33.

16. Kolko DJ, et al. Child welfare recommendations to improve mental health services for children who have experienced abuse

and neglect: a national perspective. *Adm Policy Ment Health.* 2009;36(1):50-62.

17. National Child Traumatic Stress Network. National Child Traumatic Stress Network Web site. http://www.nctsnet.org/nccts/nav.do?pid=hom_main. Accessed June 21, 2010.

18. Cohen JA, et al. The importance of culture in treating abused and neglected children: an empirical review. *Child Maltreat.* 2001;6(2):148-157.

19. Cohen JA, et al. A multisite, randomized controlled trial for children with sexual abuse-related PTSD symptoms. *J Am Acad Child Adolesc Psychiatry.* 2004;43(4):393-402.

20. Cohen JA, Mannarino AP. Factors that mediate treatment outcome of sexually abused preschool children. *J Am Acad Child Adolesc Psychiatry.* 1996;35(10):1402-1410.

21. Cohen JA, Mannarino AP. A treatment outcome study for sexually abused preschool children: initial findings. *J Am Acad Child Adolesc Psychiatry.* 1996;35(1):42-50.

22. Cohen JA, Mannarino AP. A treatment study for sexually abused preschool children: outcome during a one-year follow-up. *J Am Acad Child Adolesc Psychiatry.* 1997;36(9):1228-1235.

23. Cohen JA, Mannarino AP. Factors that mediate treatment outcome of sexually abused preschool children: six- and 12-month follow-up. *J Am Acad Child Adolesc Psychiatry.* 1998;37(1):44-51.

24. Cohen JA, Mannarino AP. Predictors of treatment outcome in sexually abused children. *Child Abuse Negl.* 2000;24(7):983-994.

25. Cohen JA, Mannarino AP. Addressing attributions in treating abused children. *Child Maltreat.* 2002;7(1):82-86.

26. Cohen JA, Mannarino AP, Knudsen K. Treating sexually abused children: 1 year follow-up of a randomized controlled trial. *Child Abuse Negl.* 2005;29(2):135-145.

27. Cohen JA, et al. A pilot randomized controlled trial of combined trauma-focused CBT and sertraline for childhood PTSD symptoms. *J Am Acad Child Adolesc Psychiatry.* 2007; 46(7):811-819.

28. Cohen JA, Mannarino AP, Rogal S. Treatment practices for childhood posttraumatic stress disorder. *Child Abuse Negl.* 2001;25(1):123-135.

29. Cohen JA, et al. Treating child abuse-related posttraumatic stress and comorbid substance abuse in adolescents. *Child Abuse Negl.* 2003;27(12):1345-1365.

30. Deblinger E, et al. A follow-up study of a multisite, randomized, controlled trial for children with sexual abuse-related PTSD symptoms. *J Am Acad Child Adolesc Psychiatry.* 2006;45(12):1474-1484.

31. Kolko DJ, et al. Community treatment of child sexual abuse: a survey of practitioners in the National Child Traumatic Stress Network. *Adm Policy Ment Health.* 2009;36(1):37-49.

32. Saywitz KJ, et al. Treatment for sexually abused children and adolescents. *Am Psychol.* 2000;55(9):1040-1049.

33. Berwick D, Godfrey A, Roessner J. *Curing Health Care.* San Francisco, CA: Jossey-Bass; 1990.

34. Berwick DM, James B, Coye MJ. Connections between quality measurement and improvement. *Med Care.* 2003;41(1 Suppl):I30-38.

Chapter 11

HOW DOCTORS AND NURSES PREVENT CHILD ABUSE

What shall I give my children? who are poor,
Who are adjudged the leastwise of the land,
Who are my sweetest lepers, who demand
No velvet and no velvety velour;
But who have begged me for a brisk contour,
Crying that they are quasi contraband
Because unfinished, graven by a hand
Less than angelic, admirable or sure.
My hand is stuffed with mode, design, device.
But I lack access to my proper stone.
And plentitude of plan shall not suffice
Nor grief nor love shall be enough alone
To ratify my little halves who bear
Across an autumn freezing everywhere.

— **Gwendolyn Brooks**, from *The Children of the Poor*

The different forms of child maltreatment require different preventive approaches. All of these approaches can be referred to as ways of "improving the childhood experience." This chapter will discuss different preventive approaches as well as the problems they present.

PREVENTION OF PHYSICAL ABUSE AND NEGLECT

Physical abuse can occur at any age; however, it is most serious and most frequent in the first 3 years of a child's life.[1] Neglect is even more concentrated into the early years, because it is defined by developmental dependency factors.

SOCIAL AND CULTURAL RISKS

Sociologists David Gil[2] and Straus[3] emphasized cultural and social factors in incidents of physical abuse and neglect, especially society's acceptance of corporal punishment as a means of controlling children and the occurrence of poverty. Korbin[4] described how the culture defines child abuse. Garbarino[5] reemphasized the importance of poverty as a risk factor for child abuse and neglect. These theories have not been sufficiently tested because of a lack of technology for the accurate, complete, and timely measurement of the prevalence of physical abuse and neglect. Furthermore, the elimination or significant reduction of poverty has not been politically feasible in the US.

Early preventive efforts identified at-risk families and offered them support from the health system.[6] These measures appeared to significantly reduce physical abuse, but neglect was still observed. Support services via home visiting and individual support to mothers became the best-studied preventive method. A model of home visiting by nurses, in which nurses helped parents and expectant parents address their own risk factors, was developed and rigorously studied for more than 20 years.[7] The program's effectiveness was clearly demonstrated by a reduction in reports of child maltreatment and of injuries in general. Still, it has not been put into general use, probably because of its high cost.

Recently, Dubowitz[8] has described a simpler and less expensive preventive methodology that can be easily incorporated into primary health care of mothers, infants, and young children and may be as effective as home visiting. In the program, Safe Environment for Every Kid (SEEK), mothers of infants and young children are asked to complete a questionnaire that screens for risk factors for child maltreatment, especially depression. The risk factors are then addressed using conventional mental health or social interventions. The program appears to be well accepted by families, and it reduces reports of child maltreatment as well as the use of harsh physical punishments by parents. It could be delivered at a low incremental cost by the existing primary health care system.

PROTECTIVE ENVIRONMENTS: LICENSED CHILDCARE
The preventive measures discussed above focus on infants and children who spend most of their time at home; however, many young children spend substantial time in childcare settings. It has been demonstrated that large, licensed daycare settings take precautions to protect their young charges and that serious or fatal injuries, whether unintentional or inflicted, are extremely rare in such centers.[9] Family daycare settings, in which providers are sometimes alone with multiple infants and children, are not as safe as large, licensed centers, but they are as safe as the average home.[10] Acts of physical abuse that cause fatal or life-threatening injury are so violent, they rarely occur when more than one adult is present.[11]

Other Benefits of Childcare
Childcare enriched with cognitive and emotional nurture can also prevent developmental problems that sometimes arise in high-risk and stressed families.[12]

PREVENTING SHAKEN BABY SYNDROME

Confessions by caregivers[11] that infants' prolonged crying drove them to shake the babies, causing brain injury, led Ronald Barr and his associates to develop a prevention program that would help parents deal with crying babies in a safer way.[13] They have demonstrated that the program effectively teaches parents about infants' crying patterns and how the crying can be safely handled. Because shaken baby syndrome (SBS) has a low incidence in the population, proof of actual prevention will require large or long-term studies; however, the practice of shaking infants to control them is not rare.[14] Although brain damage by shaking requires great force,[15] subtle brain injury might result from less violent acts, and all shaking should be avoided. Like the SEEK program, a program to prevent SBS can be integrated into existing primary health care services.

THE PREVENTION OF SEXUAL ABUSE

Until the 1970s, sexual abuse was not considered a significant health or social problem, and prevention was not undertaken. Reports made in previous eras were considered fantasies or outright lies by the children involved. With recognition of the prevalence of sexual abuse in the 1970s, prevention was undertaken in the 1980s. Wurtele summarized the situation in a 1992 book,[16] and Daro published another thorough review in 1994.[17]

Early prevention efforts usually involved providing children with information about how to avoid sexual abuse. Cordelia Anderson developed a number of presentations and published them through the Minneapolis organization Illusion Theatre.[18,19] While it was possible to prove that children as young as kindergarten age could learn the concept of self-protection,[20] it was difficult to prove that sexual abuse was actually being prevented. Furthermore, the morality of expecting young children to protect themselves aroused concerns from authorities such as Richard Krugman, who published a commentary[21] "Preventing Sexual Abuse of Children in Day Care: Whose Problem Is It Anyway?" Nevertheless, a generation of children learned the definition of sexual abuse, learned that it was wrong, and may have learned how to avoid it. The overall effect of these programs appears to have been beneficial and may be partly responsible for the recent decline in the incidence of sexual abuse.[22]

THE PROBLEM OF MEASUREMENT

Demonstration of the effectiveness of prevention programs and of prevention overall requires an ability to measure both the incidence and prevalence of the various forms of child maltreatment. Unfortunately, reliable tools for measuring the occurrence of child maltreatment have not been developed. Federal efforts in this area have been limited to the tally of child abuse reports made to departments of social services in the states and counties or to law enforcement agencies. Population surveys[23] reveal much higher rates of abuse than are suggested by compiled reports.

Prior to the passage of child abuse reporting laws in the 1960s, there were no reports to be counted. Funding became available to compile and count child abuse reports after the passage of CAPTA in 1974, and a surge was noted that was almost totally artificial in the sense that abuse cases had been occurring for a long time, but had only just begun to be reported and measured. Given this circumstance, it seems clear that only repeated surveys done with consistent definitions and methodologies can reveal trends or make it possible to compare populations. Useful and reliable measurement of child maltreatment remains a challenge in 2010, and the evaluation of prevention remains incomplete.

REFERENCES

1. Wu SS, et al. Risk factors for infant maltreatment: a population-based study. *Child Abuse Negl.* 2004;28(12):1253-1264.

2. Gil DG. Incidence of child abuse and the demographic characteristics of the persons involved. In: Helfer RE, Kempe CH, eds. *The Battered Child.* Chicago, IL: The University of Chicago Press; 1968:10-39.

3. Straus MA, Kantor GK. Stress and child abuse. In: Helfer RE, Kempe RA, eds. *The Battered Child.* Chicago, IL: The University of Chicago Press; 1987:42-59.

4. Korbin J. Culture and Child Maltreatment. In: Helfer ME, Kempe RS, Krugman, RD, eds. *The Battered Child.* Chicago, IL: The University of Chicago Press; 1997:29-48.

5. Garbarino J. The Role of Economic Deprivation in the Social Context of Child Maltreatment. In: Helfer MEK, Kempe RS, Krugman RD, eds. *The Battered Child.* Chicago, IL: The University of Chicago Press; 1997:49-60.

6. Gray JO, et al. Prediction and prevention of child abuse and neglect. *Child Abuse Negl.* 1977;1(1):45-58.

7. Olds DL. Prenatal and infancy home visiting by nurses: from randomized trials to community replication. *Prev Sci.* 2002;3(3):153-172.

8. Dubowitz H, et al. Pediatric primary care to help prevent child maltreatment: the Safe Environment for Every Kid (SEEK) model. *Pediatrics.* 2009;123(3):858-864.

9. Chadwick D, Phillips M. Safety in Numbers: Protecting Children from Death and Serious Injury by Licensed Childcare Centers. In: Alexander R, ed. *Child Fatality Review: An Interdisciplinary Guide and Photographic Reference.* St. Louis, MO: G.W. Medical Publishing Inc.; 2007:709-713.

10. Rivara FP, et al. Risk of injury to children less than 5 years of age in day care versus home care settings. *Pediatrics.* 1989;84(6):1011-1016.

11. Starling SP, et al. Analysis of perpetrator admissions to inflicted traumatic brain injury in children. *Arch Pediatr Adolesc Med.* 2004;158(5):454-458.

12. Ramey CT, et al. Persistent effects of early childhood education on high-risk children and their mothers. *Appl Develop Sci.* 2000;4(1):2-14.

13. Barr RG, et al. Effectiveness of educational materials designed to change knowledge and behaviors regarding crying and shaken-baby syndrome in mothers of newborns: a randomized, controlled trial. *Pediatrics.* 2009;123(3):972-980.

14. Theodore AD, et al. Epidemiologic features of the physical and sexual maltreatment of children in the Carolinas. *Pediatrics.* 2005;115(3):e331-337.

15. American Academy of Pediatrics. Shaken Baby Syndrome: Rotational Cranial Injuries—Technical Report (T0039). *Pediatrics.* 2001;108(1):206-210.

16. Wurtele SK, Miller-Perrin CL, Melton GB. *Preventing child sexual abuse: sharing the responsibility.* Lincoln, NE: University of Nebraska Press; 1992.

17. Daro DA. Prevention of child sexual abuse. *Future Child.* 1994;4(2):198-223.

18. Kent C. *No Easy Answers: A Sexual Abuse Prevention Curriculum for Junior and Senior High Students.* Minneapolis, MN: Illusion Theater; 1982.

19. Anderson C. *Child Sexual Abuse Prevention: How to Take the First Steps.* Minneapolis, MN: Illusion Theater; 1983.

20. Blumberg EJ, et al. The touch discrimination component of sexual abuse prevention training: Unanticipated positive consequences. *J Interpersonal Violence.* 1991;6(1):12-28.

21. Krugman RD. Preventing sexual abuse of children in day care: whose problem is it anyway? *Pediatrics.* 1985;75(6):1150-1151.

22. Jones LM, Finkelhor D, Kopiec K. Why is sexual abuse declining? A survey of state child protection administrators. *Child Abuse Negl.* 2001;25(9):1139-1158.

23. MacMillan HL, et al. Prevalence of child physical and sexual abuse in the community. Results from the Ontario Health Supplement. *JAMA.* 1997;278(2):131-135.

Chapter 12

CHILD ABUSE DOCTORS IN THE UNITED KINGDOM

England and America are two countries separated by the same language.

— **George Bernard Shaw**

Any American author's view of the development of child abuse medicine in the United Kingdom (UK) is likely to be incomplete. But it is a small world—and particularly small for speakers of the English language. Much knowledge and many problems are shared.

THE FIRST STIRRINGS

Auguste Ambroise Tardieu's description of physical abuse in 1860 references British Member of Parliament Michael Thomas Sadler's efforts to improve the situation of children in the Kingdom.[1] A societal recognition of child abuse appears to have surfaced in the UK toward the end of the 19th century—the same time that the problem was attracting attention in the US. The (British) National Society for the Prevention of Cruelty to Children (NSPCC) was founded in 1884 by Liverpool banker Thomas Agnew, who copied the New York model,[2] but the early efforts did not involve medical doctors.

EARLY AND IMPORTANT MEDICAL CONTRIBUTIONS

As in the US, the medical consciousness of child abuse in the UK appears to have been awakened by the work of C. Henry Kempe. He sought colleagues in many countries, including the UK, and some of them joined him in founding the International Society for the Prevention of Child Abuse and Neglect (ISPCAN). They diagnosed child abuse and treated children and families.

Pediatrician Margaret Lynch was an important early contributor to British child abuse medicine and has continued to publish on the subject for decades.[3-23] Her follow-up study of 40 families who were given intensive family care after an occurrence of physical child abuse[24] is classic. Carried out at a children's psychiatric inpatient unit (The Park Hospital in Oxford) with nearby residential facilities for families, the study concludes that family-based interventions after the occurrence of abuse are difficult and not always effective. She emphasizes that prevention of physical child abuse, rather than intervention after the fact, should be the priority.

Psychiatrist David Jones was also an early contributor. He spent a sabbatical year at the Kempe Center in Colorado, which led to useful collaboration,[25-27] and was also part of the Oxford faculty. Jones observed that some families were "untreatable" with available methods and described these families' characteristics. This observation came as no surprise to child abuse doctors and child protection social workers.

Later, Jones and Lynch[28] and Harvey Marcovitch[29] authored commentaries supporting the landmark observations of David Southall about the deliberate suffocation of children by their caregivers. They pointed out the great importance of confronting the deceit that accompanies certain forms of child maltreatment.

DAVID SOUTHALL'S INTOLERABLE CONCLUSIONS

Southall's observations had been made using covert video surveillance (CVS) in a hospital. His use of this technology may have provoked attacks, which culminated in his being stricken from the list of licensed medical doctors in the UK by the General Medical Council (GMC).[30] Marcovitch[29] states,

"...one consequence of diagnostic uncertainty in all forms of maltreatment has been an epidemic of complaints against pediatricians, fuelled by campaigners, journalists, and legislators who are convinced that misdiagnosis is common. More sinister than complaints has been a pattern of threats, physical attacks, stalking, and public allegations that doctors themselves are child abusers."

The pattern Marcovitch describes led to suppression of pediatric work against child abuse.[31]

Concerns about the possibility of suffocation as a cause of sudden infant death had existed for many years. Southall's videos proved beyond doubt that this phenomenon occurred, and although infrequent, purposeful suffocation of children by parents and caretakers was far from rare[32,33]; indeed, his findings were soon corroborated by similar studies in the US.[34] For some of the British, this was an intolerable conclusion. Doctors who opposed the use of CVS contended that some of the videos that caught parents suffocating babies were of poor quality, and pointed out that Southall had not made control videos of known nonabusive parents.[35] Southall's work had preceded the development of the tiny, concealable video cameras that produce high-quality images. The use of CVS does raise ethical questions, and it requires the employment of carefully designed protocols[34]; however, concern for parents' privacy is clearly overridden when a child's life is at stake, which is typically the case when CVS is used. The recommendation for a controlled study of CVS is contrived. A study of this sort could not be approved by a human subjects research review committee.

Sir Roy Meadow's Discovery

British psychiatrist Richard Asher coined the term "Munchausen syndrome" to describe the condition of persons who repeatedly sought unnecessary medical care for faked maladies.[36] Asher derived the term from the Baron von Munchausen, an 18th-century storyteller whose sensational tales have been collected and published under the title *The Surprising Adventures of Baron Munchausen*. Like many medical eponyms, Munchausen syndrome fails to provide much useful information about the condition it names. It nonetheless became widely accepted in and after the 1950s.

In 1977, pediatrician Roy Meadow published an article describing cases in which parents repeatedly faked illness in their children with harmful results.[36] Meadow named the disorder Munchausen syndrome by proxy (MSBP), and again, the term gained popularity. More cases were soon described by other authors, and in 1987, Donna Rosenberg was able to summarize findings from about 100 cases,[37] 9 of which had been fatal for the child. Serious harm had occurred in all cases, and it was clear that this syndrome was a form of child abuse, regardless of the motivation of the parent or caregiver, who faked illness in the child. In some cases, the illness was faked by providing a false history, and in others, the parent induced it. When the parent induced illness, some children died as a result, and when the illness was faked by a false history, the child was often subjected to unnecessary medical procedures. The syndrome consisted of caregiver and doctor behavior, not a caregiver psychiatric condition. Most cases required unwitting collaboration by doctors, especially pediatric subspecialists, who, fooled by the parents' clever mimicking or production of illness in the child, pursued various diagnoses often at length.

Meadow's formulation of this dangerous form of child abuse elicited considerable political opposition. In the House of Lords in October 2001, Earl Howe[38] made a speech about it, emphasizing the problem of misdiagnosis by unskilled workers. Howe's statement was interpreted by members of the press and by some advocates as a denial of the existence of MSBP; however, clinical observations continued to be made in the UK, the US, and other countries,[39-47] leaving little doubt that the condition occurs in many cultures and in a form that repeats itself sufficiently to require a medical diagnostic label.

The naming of this condition has been a subject of ongoing discussion.[48] Psychiatrists claimed it for their diagnostic and statistical manual (DSM) under the name "factitious disorder by proxy." A serious problem with psychiatric conceptualization of the behavior is that few of the suspected parents allow themselves to be properly evaluated, and forced psychiatric evaluation may not be useful in this condition. Before organizing a coercive intervention, the parents' involvement in the child's illness must first be proven. A psychiatric diagnosis in the abusing parent is not necessary. Thomas Roesler and Carole Jenny renamed the condition "medical child abuse" in their recent book.[49] This appears eminently sensible.

Some cases of MSBP involved the recurrent partial suffocation of infants or children who would be presented for care while recovering from induced airway obstruction. In addition, airway obstruction continued to the point of death might also mimic sudden infant death syndrome (SIDS), and this was pointed out by Meadow.[50] It was because of this published work that Meadow was recruited as an expert witness in the case of *Regina v Clark* described in *Chapter 8*. This, in turn, led to the baseless prosecution committed by the GMC, leading to the striking of Meadow and Southall from the doctors' registry.[30] This was accompanied by a media campaign of vilification.

Meadow is famous for a number of accomplishments. He was a leader in the process of elevating the British Pediatric Association to the status of a Royal College of Pediatrics and Child Health, co-drafting the petition to Queen Elizabeth II requesting consideration for the College's Royal charter. As a result of all of his distinguished work, he was knighted.

RECOGNIZING BRAIN DAMAGE FROM SHAKING: SHAKEN BABY SYNDROME

A. Norman Guthkelch, the first British pediatric neurosurgeon,[51] made a landmark observation in 1971. He reviewed literature up to that point in time and described 2 cases in which a parent gave a history of shaking an infant just prior to the infant's loss of consciousness and with subsequent diagnosis of subdural hematoma and brain swelling. Adding this clinical data to the experimental observations of Alexander Ommaya,[52] Guthkelch concluded that shaking a baby without impact could produce brain injury and subdural hematoma. Within the next 3 years, John Caffey published 2 articles, which named the new condition the "whiplash shaken infant syndrome" and added additional, confessed cases in which shaking produced brain damage and subdural hematoma.[53,54]

Knowledge of shaken baby syndrome (SBS) still rests largely on confessions of caregivers, and these have been well studied in recent years.[55] A suitable animal model available for experimentation has not been found, and biomechanical analyses still lack sufficient data about the real injury tolerance of infants and children. These gaps allow skeptics to challenge the fact that shaking produces brain damage.

The shaking of young children for disciplinary reasons has been acknowledged by about 3% of mothers in a US sample,[56] and a few instances of shaking have been captured on security cameras used by parents to monitor childcare providers, but all of the shaken children captured on video escaped serious injury.

MIXED BLESSINGS—VALUABLE UK PUBLICATIONS WITH FLAWS

Chris Hobbs' study on skull fractures[57] is an example of an important article flawed by a single rash sentence. Hobbs' article provides important observations about the relationship between skull fracture severity and complexity and the type and degree of force required and thereby to the likelihood of a non-accidental mechanism. Unfortunately, the article also contains a statement that "…the diagnosis of child abuse requires absolute certainty." Although the statement is plainly wrong, it has been seized upon and quoted by doctors who express skepticism about the principle that serious brain injuries in infants and children generally require force applied to the head.[58] To these skeptics, a requirement for "absolute" certainty is desirable.

Observations by Hobbs about reflex anal dilatation as a sign of past anal penetration[59,60] led to substantial overdiagnosis of sexual abuse which, in turn, led to the Cleveland Inquiry,[61] which was a difficult experience for British child abuse doctors, many of whom were criticized.

Another example of "mixed blessings" is Geddes' research on inflicted head injuries.[62] This work focused on an important clinical observation made in many cases—the initial presentation of infants with apnea or impaired respiration. Geddes examined the brainstem and the cranial cervical junction of the spinal cord and medulla and, in some cases, found evidence of damage. However, the work led to the generalization that a relatively minor event might launch a fatal cascade with apnea leading to hypoxic-ischemic brain damage, causing subdural hematoma and retinal hemorrhages.[62] It has been shown subsequently that hypoxia alone does not produce subdural hemorrhage.[63]

BRITISH ACHIEVEMENTS

The overall achievements of child abuse doctors in the UK are outstanding. In addition to the contributions mentioned above, it is important to take note of the work of Danya Glaser,[51,64-70] Allison Kemp,[69,71-90] and many others. A comprehensive review of British child abuse medicine awaits the efforts of a native author.

REFERENCES

1. Tardieu A. *Étude médico-légale sur les attentats aux mœurs*. Paris, FR: Librairie JB Baillière et Fils; 1857.

2. National Society for the Prevention of Cruelty to Children. History of the NSPCC Child abuse - an invisible social evil. NSPCC Web site. http://www.nspcc.org.uk/. Accessed in 2009.

3. Skuse DH, et al. Failure to thrive and the risk of child abuse: a prospective population survey. *J Med Screen*. 1995;2(3):145-149.

4. Scanlon TJ, et al. Street children in Latin America. *BMJ*. 1998;316(7144):1596-600.

5. Scanlon TJ, et al. Child labour. *Br Med J*. 2002;325(7361):401-403.

6. Roberts J, Lynch MA, Golding J. Postneonatal mortality in children from abusing families. *Br Med J*. 1980;281(6233):102-104.

7. Roberts J, et al. Is there a link between cot death and child abuse? *Br Med J* (Clin Res Ed). 1984;289(6448):789-791.

8. Roberts J, et al. Prevention of child abuse: group therapy for mothers and children. *Practitioner*. 1977;219(1309):111-115.

9. Nesbitt A, Lynch MA. African children in Britain. *Arch Dis Child*. 1992;67(11):1402-1405.

10. Mrazek PJ, Lynch MA, Bentovim A. Sexual abuse of children in the United Kingdom. *Child Abuse Negl*. 1983;7(2):147-153.

11. Lynch MA, Roberts J. Predicting child abuse: signs of bonding failure in the maternity hospital. *Br Med J*. 1977;1(6061):624-626.

12. Lynch MA. A judicial comment on temporary brittle bone disease. *Arch Dis Child*. 1995;73(4):379.

13. Lynch MA. Child abuse before Kempe: an historical literature review. *Child Abuse Negl*. 1985;9(1):7-15.

14. Lynch MA. Recognizing a child at increased risk of abuse. *Paediatr.* 1979;8(4):188-199.

15. Lynch MA. The prognosis of child abuse. *J Child Psychol Psychiatry.* 1978;19(2):175-180.

16. Lynch MA. Child abuse: the family - one way to see that they need help. *Nurs Times.* 1978;74(6):suppl 38-39.

17. Lynch MA. Ill-health and child abuse. *Lancet.* 1975;2(7929): 317-319.

18. Khan NZ, Lynch MA. Recognizing child maltreatment in Bangladesh. *Child Abuse Negl.* 1997;21(8):815-818.

19. Hesketh T, Hong ZS, Lynch MA. Child abuse in China: the views and experiences of child health professionals. *Child Abuse Negl.* 2000;24(6):867-872.

20. Hall D, Lynch MA. Violence begins at home. Domestic strife has lifelong effects on children. *Br Med J.* 1998;316(7144):1551.

21. Glaser D, Lynch MA. The medical examination of sexually abused children. *Br Med J* (Clin Res Ed). 1985;290(6475): 1145.

22. Elliman D, Lynch MA. The physical punishment of children. *Arch Dis Child.* 2000; 83(3):196-198.

23. Beswick K, Lynch MA, Roberts J. General practice observed. Child abuse and general practice. *Br Med J.* 1976;2(6039):800-802.

24. Lynch M, Roberts J. *Consequences of child abuse.* Ann Arbor, MI: Academic Press, University of Michigan; 1982.

25. Jones DP, The untreatable family. *Child Abuse Negl.* 1987; 11(3):409-420.

26. Jones DP, Krugman RD. Can a three-year-old child bear witness to her sexual assault and attempted murder? *Child Abuse Negl.* 1986;10(2):253-258.

27. Oates RK, et al. Erroneous concerns about child sexual abuse. *Child Abuse Negl.* 2000; 24(1):149-157.

28. Jones DP, Lynch MA. Diagnosing and responding to serious child abuse. Confronting deceit and denial is vital if children are to be protected. *BMJ.* 1998;317(7157):484-485.

29. Marcovitch H, Jones DP. Protecting abused children. *Lancet.* 2007;369(9576):1844-1846.

30. Chadwick DL, Krous HF, Runyan DK. Meadow, Southall, and the General Medical Council of the United Kingdom. *Pediatrics.* 2006;117(6):2247-2251.

31. Williams C. United Kingdom General Medical Council fails child protection. *Pediatrics.* 2007;119(4):800-802.

32. Southall DP, et al. Apnoeic episodes induced by smothering: two cases identified by covert video surveillance. *Br Med J.* 1987;294(6588):1637-1641.

33. Southall DP, et al. Covert video recordings of life-threatening child abuse: lessons for child protection. *Pediatrics.* 1997; 100(5):735-760.

34. Hall DE, et al. Evaluation of covert video surveillance in the diagnosis of Munchausen syndrome by proxy: lessons from 41 cases. *Pediatrics.* 2000;105(6):1305-1312.

35. David TJ. Spying on mothers [letter; comment]. *Lancet.* 1994;344(8915):133.

36. Meadow R. Munchausen syndrome by proxy. The hinterland of child abuse. *Lancet.* 1977;2(8033):343-345.

37. Rosenberg DA. Web of deceit: a literature review of Munchausen syndrome by proxy [see comments]. *Child Abuse Negl.* 1987;11(4):547-563.

38. House of Lords. Daily Hansard. UK Parliament Web site. http://www.publications.parliament.uk/pa/ld200102/ldhansrd/vo011017/text/11017-06.htm. Published October 17, 2001. Accessed April 26, 2009.

39. Sahin F, et al. Munchausen syndrome by proxy: a case report. *Turk J Pediatr.* 2002;44(4):334-338.

40. Bartsch C, et al. Munchausen syndrome by proxy (MSBP): an extreme form of child abuse with a special forensic challenge. *Forensic Sci Int.* 2003;137(2-3):147-151.

41. Bennett AM, et al. Spitting in the ear: a falsified disease using video evidence. *J Laryngol Otol.* 2005;119(11):926-927.

42. Jovanovic AA, et al. Munchausen syndrome by proxy [in Serbian]. *Srp Arh Celok Lek.* 2005;133(34):173-179.

43. Vennemann B, et al. Suffocation and poisoning—the hard-hitting side of Munchausen syndrome by proxy. *Int J Legal Med.* 2005;119(2):98-102.

44. Birmingham CL, Sidhu FK. An algorithm for the diagnosis of Munchausen's syndrome in eating disorders. *Eat Weight Disord.* 2007;12(4):e75-77.

45. Hassler F, Zamorski H, Weirich S. The problem of differentiating between sudden infant death syndrome, fatal Munchausen's syndrome by proxy, and infanticide [in German]. *Z Kinder Jugendpsychiatr Psychother.* 2007;35(4):237-244; quiz 245-246.

46. Fujiwara T, et al. Differences of Munchausen syndrome by proxy according to predominant symptoms in Japan. *Pediatr Int.* 2008;50(4):537-540.

47. Al-Haidar FA. Munchausen syndrome by proxy and child's rights. *Saudi Med J.* 2008; 29(3):452-454.

48. Ayoub CC, et al. Position paper: definitional issues in Munchausen by proxy. *Child Maltreat.* 2002;7(2):105-111.

49. Roesler T, Jenny C. *Medical Child Abuse: Beyond Munchausen Syndrome by Proxy.* Elk Grove Village, IL: American Academy of Pediatrics; 2008.

50. Meadow R. Suffocation, recurrent apnea, and sudden infant death. *J Pediatr.* 1990; 117(3):351-357.

51. Guthkelch AN. Infantile subdural hematoma and its relationship to whiplash injuries. *Br Med J.* 1971;2:430-431.

52. Ommaya AK, Yarnell P. Subdural haematoma after whiplash injury. *Lancet.* 1969;2(7614):237-239.

53. Caffey J. On the theory and practice of shaking infants. Its potential residual effects of permanent brain damage and mental retardation. *Am J Dis Child.* 1972;124(2):161-169.

54. Caffey J. The whiplash shaken infant syndrome: manual shaking by the extremities with whiplash-induced intracranial and intraocular bleedings, linked with residual permanent brain damage and mental retardation. *Pediatrics.* 1974;54(4):396-403.

55. Starling SP, et al. Analysis of perpetrator admissions to inflicted traumatic brain injury in children. *Arch Pediatr Adolesc Med.* 2004;158(5):454-458.

56. Theodore AD, et al. Epidemiologic features of the physical and sexual maltreatment of children in the Carolinas. *Pediatrics.* 2005;115(3):e331-337.

57. Hobbs CJ. Skull fracture and the diagnosis of abuse. *Arch Dis Child.* 1984;59(3):246-252.

58. Ommaya AK, Goldsmith W, Thibault L. Biomechanics and neuropathology of adult and paediatric head injury. *Br J Neurosurg.* 2002;16(3):220-242.

59. Hobbs CJ, Wynne JM. Diagnosing sexual abuse. *Lancet.* 1987;2(8573):1455.

60. Hobbs CJ, Wynne JM. Buggery in childhood—a common syndrome of child abuse. *Lancet.* 1986;2(8510):792-796.

61. Summary of the Cleveland inquiry. *BMJ.* 1988;297(6642):190-191.

62. Geddes JF, Whitwell HL. Inflicted head injury in infants. *Forensic Sci Int.* 2004;146(2-3):83-88.

63. Byard RW, et al. Lack of evidence for a causal relationship between hypoxic-ischemic encephalopathy and subdural hemorrhage in fetal life, infancy, and early childhood. *Pediatr Dev Pathol.* 2007;10(5):348-350.

64. Trowell J, et al. Psychotherapy for sexually abused girls: psychopathological outcome findings and patterns of change. *Br J Psychiatry.* 2002;180:234-247.

65. Glaser D, Collins C. The response of young, non-sexually abused children to anatomically correct dolls. *J Child Psychol Psychiatry.* 1989;30(4):547-560.

66. Glaser D. Emotional abuse and neglect (psychological maltreatment): a conceptual framework. *Child Abuse Negl.* 2002;26(6-7):697-714.

67. Glaser D. Child abuse and neglect and the brain—a review. *J Child Psychol Psychiatry.* 2000;41(1):97-116.

68. Glaser D. Treatment issues in child sexual abuse. *Br J Psychiatry.* 1991;159:769-782.

69. Gilbert R, et al. Recognizing and responding to child maltreatment. *Lancet.* 2009; 373(9658):167-180.

70. Brandon S, et al. Recovered memories of childhood sexual abuse. Implications for clinical practice. *Br J Psychiatry.* 1998;172:296-307.

71. Barnes PM, et al. Abdominal injury due to child abuse. *Lancet.* 2005;366(9481):234-235.

72. Datta S, et al. Neuroradiological aspects of subdural haemorrhages. *Arch Dis Child*. 2005;90(9):947-951.

73. Dunstan FD, et al. A scoring system for bruise patterns: a tool for identifying abuse. *Arch Dis Child*. 2002;86(5):330-333.

74. Ellaway BA, et al. Are abused babies protected from further abuse? *Arch Dis Child*. 2004;89(9):845-846.

75. Jayawant S, et al. Subdural haemorrhages in infants: population based study. *BMJ*. 1998; 317(7172):1558-1561.

76. Kemp A, et al. Can we identify abusive bites on children? *Arch Dis Child*. 2006;91(11): 951.

77. Kemp AM. Investigating subdural haemorrhages in infants. *Arch Dis Child*. 2002;86(2):98-102.

78. Kemp AM, et al. Which radiological investigations should be performed to identify fractures in suspected child abuse? *Clin Radiol*. 2006;61(9):723-736.

79. Kemp AM, et al. Patterns of skeletal fractures in child abuse: systematic review. *BMJ*. 2008;337:a1518.

80. Kemp AM, Mott AM, Sibert JR. Accidents and child abuse in bathtub submersions. *Arch Dis Child*. 1994;70(5):435-438.

81. Kemp AM, Sibert J. The shaken infant syndrome. Deal with minor episodes of abuse to prevent more serious injuries. *BMJ*. 1995;310(6994):1600; author reply 1600-1601.

82. Kemp AM, et al. Apnoea and brain swelling in non-accidental head injury. *Arch Dis Child*. 2003;88(6):472-476; discussion 472-476.

83. Maguire S, et al. Diagnosing abuse: a systematic review of torn frenum and other intra-oral injuries. *Arch Dis Child*. 2007; 92(12):1113-1117.

84. Maguire S, et al. Does cardiopulmonary resuscitation cause rib fractures in children? A systematic review. *Child Abuse Negl*. 2006;30(7):739-751.

85. Maguire S, et al. Are there patterns of bruising in childhood which are diagnostic or suggestive of abuse? A systematic review. *Arch Dis Child*. 2005;90(2):182-186.

86. Paranjothy S, et al. The incidence and aetiology of epistaxis in infants: a population-based study. *Arch Dis Child*. 2009.

87. Prosser I, et al. How old is this fracture? Radiologic dating of fractures in children: a systematic review. *AJR Am J Roentgenol.* 2005;184(4):1282-1286.

88. Sibert JR, Maguire SA, Kemp AM. How good is the evidence available in child protection? *Arch Dis Child.* 2007;92(2):107-108.

89. Sibert JR, et al. The incidence of severe physical child abuse in Wales. *Child Abuse Negl.* 2002;26(3):267-276.

90. Yeoh C, et al. Patterns of scald injuries. *Arch Dis Child.* 1994;71(2):156-158.

Chapter 13

DOCTORS' STORIES: A-C

The stories that comprise this and the following chapters are about the "early adopters" of child abuse medicine, who were often engaged in academic medicine rather than private practice. Only their most important published work is cited in these biographical chapters, but much more of it is cited elsewhere in the book.

DOCTORS' VIEWS OF CHILD ABUSE

All doctors are likely to see patients who have been abused, but many doctors are unlikely to recognize abuse. Until recently, interpersonal violence and abuse were not a part of medical school curricula, and although experience taught doctors that these acts cause medical problems, medical remedies were not at hand. The time may come when all primary care doctors are able to inquire about abuse skillfully in the course of routine care, including the care of adults, many of whom may have been abused as children. One essential characteristic of a child abuse doctor is that he or she recognizes abuse when the patient exhibits signs or symptoms.

Different medical specialists encounter child abuse in different ways. Family physicians and pediatricians provide most of the medical care to infants and children, and in the US, the health care of children is divided about equally between these 2 types of doctors. Both types inevitably encounter abused children, who may or may not demonstrate signs of abuse at the time they are seen.

GENERAL PEDIATRICS

Most general pediatricians do not emphasize child abuse in their practices, but have encountered recognizable cases, simply because they provide health care to children. Of course, much of the abuse affecting children in their practices does not produce visible or tangible findings, and many abused children never complain, particularly when they are young. Pediatricians handle child abuse cases with some discomfort and varying responses.[1]

SHERMAN WOLDMAN: TYPICAL EXPERIENCE OF A GENERAL PEDIATRICIAN

Sherman Woldman completed a pediatric residency at the Buffalo Children's Hospital around 1958, before C. Henry Kempe had published. He provides the following anecdote about a typical experience for his era:

"My earliest recognition of suspected child abuse was during my pediatric residency in 1957 or 1958. An infant repeatedly came to the ER with reported 'accidental' trauma. As I recall, at various times, he came in with 1) vomiting due to a 'fall'" with an abdominal contusion, 2) a fractured forearm and multiple bruises, 3) facial bruises. He had been sent to our ER on at least one occasion from a community hospital for trauma care. Even though we suspected abuse, we were told we could not report it anywhere or the hospital could be sued. We eventually found out that he had showed up DOA (dead on arrival) at a community hospital."

Woldman also describes seeing a 12-year-old girl with a genital injury that, in retrospect, was probably abusive, but at the time, was attributed to a "bicycle injury." After the New York child abuse reporting law was passed, he reported several cases of physical abuse, none of which were fatal, and the children's parents did not sue him.

Just prior to his retirement in 2007, Woldman received a confession from a mother in his practice that all of her daughters had been incestuously abused. At that point, they were all over 18, and the child abuse reporting law no longer applied to them.

OTHER SPECIALISTS
Psychiatrists might have been expected to take an interest in child abuse, but they were slow to enter the field, likely because Sigmund Freud led the discipline in the wrong direction. The specialty of emergency medicine grew out of pediatrics and general practice, and doctors in emergency departments have frequently concentrated their interest on child abuse because they inevitably see so many cases.

Pathologists, who became medical examiners for local or state governments, would be involved automatically in fatal child abuse cases; however, only a few of them took sufficient interest to publish about child abuse or attend early medical conferences emphasizing the problem, much less attempted to set standards for their specialty. Medical examiners are not necessarily child abuse doctors, although they should be. Some pediatric pathologists focused their work on child abuse, while some specifically focused on sudden infant death syndrome (SIDS) and the possible overlapping of the 2 problems.

Early descriptions of serious physical abuse often involved cases with multiple fractures of extremities, ribs, and the skull; therefore, radiologists, particularly pediatric radiologists, were frequently involved in the diagnosis and definition of cases. As in the case of medical examiners, the radiologists' involvement was *ex officio* and often unsought by the individual doctor. The early—but abortive—

work of John Caffey and Frederick Silverman is described in *Chapter 3*.

THE ICE BREAKERS: CHILD ABUSE MEDICINE BEFORE 1980

The 2 "true innovators" for the field of child abuse medicine were Auguste Ambroise Tardieu in 1860 and Kempe in 1962 (see *Chapter 1* and *Chapter 3*). Tardieu was first by about a century, but Kempe did not cite the former's work when he wrote the battered child article and seems to have been unaware of it. There was no intervening continuity of medical attention; therefore, by the 1950s when Kempe began to recognize cases of child abuse, Tardieu's work had faded into obscurity.

Freud must also be mentioned as an innovator for his original recognition of the importance of sexual abuse in 1896; however, his recantation had a dampening effect on the field from which it is just beginning to dry.

DOCTORS' STORIES

For organizational purposes, the following entries are arranged in alphabetical order.

JOYCE ADAMS, PEDIATRICIAN

After a pediatric residency at the Montefiore Hospital and Medical Center in New York City, Joyce Adams **(Figure 13-1)** won a National Health Service Corps scholarship, requiring her to work in an inner city neighborhood health center, which she did in Kansas City, Missouri. In 1981, she encountered an 8-year-old boy who presented with painful urination and a yellow-green discharge from his penis. After correctly diagnosing his symptoms as gonorrhea, she discovered the boy had acquired the infection from an 11-year-old girl, who had acquired it from an adult. Adams was surprised and upset when other doctors in the clinic denied the likelihood of sexual abuse as a source of a sexually transmitted disease in a child. Suzanne Sgroi wrote about this problem in 1979 (See *Chapter 5*), but there was little else in the literature at the time.

Figure 13-1

Adams shared her experience with the special interest group for child abuse in pediatrics that was growing from the listserv started by Ann Botash. She soon became involved in the developing Section on Child Abuse and Neglect (SOCAN) of the American Academy of Pediatrics (AAP) and moved to the University of Kansas Medical Center, where she joined a child protection team.

After learning of John McCann's work on defining normal genital findings in prepubertal girls, Adams moved to Fresno, California in

1988 to join in his work. As a result, their work—and that of others—led to the capability of distinguishing findings that indicated injury from abuse or other causes. Adams' research led to many publications, including an article that vividly describes the emotional price paid by professionals who work with abused children.[2]

Because of Kempe's leadership, interest in and concentration on child abuse developed more rapidly in pediatrics than in family medicine. No leader comparable to Kempe emerged from any other medical specialty.

RANDELL ALEXANDER, PEDIATRICIAN

Figure 13-2

Studying at Michigan State University, Randell Alexander (**Figure 13-2**) set out to become an experimental developmental psychologist, but was diverted to pediatric medicine and then to child abuse by Ray E. Helfer. In this process, he acquired a PhD in psychology along with his doctorate in medicine. Alexander was appointed to the Department of Pediatrics at the University of Iowa expressly to direct a child abuse program that was housed in the Division of Developmental Disabilities, and he quickly took an interest in the complexities of abusive physical injuries, especially injuries to the head and brain.

In 1984, Alexander teamed up with Helfer and radiologist Tom Slovis to describe extremity fractures, identical to those that occurred in child abuse, resulting from range-of-motion exercises used on small, premature infants to treat muscle tightness.[3] This article was very important because it provided objective documentation of exactly how these previously puzzling extremity fractures can occur and also provided a cautionary observation for the treatment of premature infants. The article on fractures was an early effort, presaging prolific contributions to the child abuse medical journal literature and several edited books. Alexander's contributions deal with all forms of child maltreatment. He has been influential in defining the syndromes of inflicted head injury.

SHIRLEY ANDERSON, PEDIATRICIAN

Shirley Anderson left her private practice of pediatrics to join McCann at Harborview Hospital in 1971. In the same year, Seattle Rape Relief, an advocacy group, succeeded in convincing Harborview Hospital authorities to establish a special medical service for rape victims, which became known as the Sexual Assault Center. This was the first such medical center in the US, and Anderson developed special services for child victims of sexual abuse. The Kempe Center in Colorado had not yet offered services for sexual abuse, and Sgroi's handbook would not be published for another 7 years. Anderson wrote protocols for interviews and medical examinations of children and for the collection of specimens that might be used as evidence in sexual abuse cases. These protocols were adopted by Seattle area law enforcement and social service agencies and used in the multi-disciplinary evaluation of child sexual abuse cases.

Only a little of Anderson's work was published,[4] but she still became well known in the field and was able to secure funding for services and training. Carole Jenny and Astrid Heger both trained with Anderson and then moved on to develop medical centers for child abuse in Providence and Los Angeles. The famous social worker Lucy Berliner was also associated with the Sexual Assault Center at Harborview Hospital and began her extensive work interviewing and treating child sexual abuse victims. Anderson's program always emphasized the need for multidisciplinary and multiagency coordination in dealing with child sexual abuse cases. Anderson continued to speak and to provide training to medical and other disciplines well into the 1990s, and the child abuse programs at Harborview Medical Center, as it is now known, remain exemplary.

RONALD BARR, PEDIATRICIAN

Ronald Barr migrated to child abuse work after establishing himself as a developmental pediatrician and a world authority on infant crying patterns. Confessions by caregivers of infants with very serious inflicted head injuries often suggested that prolonged crying had precipitated the violent shaking that was believed to cause severe brain damage. The prolonged crying of infants had been recognized for centuries as a medical problem and had generated innumerable theories, most of which were proven incorrect by Barr and his associates.

Barr pointed out that while infants demonstrated substantial variations in crying patterns, it was possible to see a peak in crying duration at around 2 months of age that tapered off as babies became older. The incidence of shaken baby syndrome in California appeared to follow the same curve for age as the pattern of infants' crying intensity. This fact, in addition to information from confessions, suggested that the prevention of shaken baby syndrome might be achieved if parents' tolerance for the crying of their babies could be increased. Since it had already been proven that there was usually no medical cause for prolonged infant crying, it seemed that there was little that could be done to reduce crying beyond what most parents were already doing. Barr and his associates developed a program that would help parents understand and tolerate their crying babies. They have demonstrated that parents learn from this program and that it is harmless.

JAN BAYS, PEDIATRICIAN

Jan Bays completed a pediatric residency at the University of California, San Diego (UCSD) School of Medicine in the late 1970s. During her residency, she was shocked by the appearance of a young child with a serious, inflicted facial and head injury. After seeing the developing Center for Child Protection at the nearby Children's Hospital of San Diego, Bays later modeled the center she developed at the Emanuel Hospital in Portland, Oregon after it. She acquired the necessary knowledge and skill for diagnosis of and intervention in all forms of child maltreatment and applied these to the development of the sophisticated center at Emanuel Hospital.

Bays was also able to make significant contributions to knowledge about child maltreatment. Notably, Bays may be the only child abuse medical doctor who is also a Buddhist monk.

RACHEL BERGER, PEDIATRICIAN

Working in a historically distinguished child abuse program at the Children's Hospital in Pittsburgh, Rachel Berger has made major contributions to the field. Her work has concentrated on the use of chemical markers in blood and spinal fluid, which could diagnose clinically unapparent, inflicted head injuries.[5] Subtle brain injuries may cause enzymes from nerve cells to escape into the blood in measurable amounts that allow recognition of sub-clinical brain injury. Widespread adoption of these techniques would probably increase the recognition rate for inflicted head injury.

CAROL BERKOWITZ, PEDIATRICIAN

Figure 13-3

In the 1970s, Carol Berkowitz **(Figure 13-3)** was on the University of California, Los Angeles (UCLA) medical school faculty based at the Harbor-UCLA medical center. Since the 1960s, a number of physically abused infants and young children required admission to the Harbor Hospital and consultation by doctors willing to recognize abusive injuries. In 1980, she became aware that many underweight infants were being seen in her facility. She opened a clinic for infants with "failure to thrive" (a blanket term applied to infants who were underweight; under the normal length; delayed in psychomotor development; or behind in all 3 parameters). The clinic focused the attention of doctors and developmental specialists on the diagnosis and care of such infants. In some cases, the infants' problems were found to result from neglect. These cases often required interventions by public social services and, sometimes, foster care. Thus, Berkowitz became a child abuse doctor and developed a relationship with the social services in her area. As sexual abuse began to be recognized more frequently, children who were suspected of being abused were also brought to Berkowitz's clinic for forensic interviews and medical examinations, and she developed a service for all forms of child maltreatment. She published extensively, emphasizing deprivation and complex problems of infants, demonstrating atypical development. Berkowitz was also very active in her medical school and in the AAP, eventually becoming its president.

ROBERT BLOCK

After the completion of a pediatric residency in Philadelphia followed by military service, Robert Block joined the faculty of a growing medical school in Oklahoma City, practicing general pediatrics and adolescent medicine. He soon joined a multidisciplinary child abuse prevention program, providing wrap-around services for families at-risk for abuse. The Oklahoma State Department of Child Welfare soon recognized him as the state medical expert on child abuse, and he began to provide case consultation for social services and law enforcement agencies throughout Oklahoma. As funding became available and the state's child abuse programs expanded, Block became more involved in child abuse work. He made major contributions to child abuse literature and also became chair of the pediatric department at the University of Oklahoma School of Medicine.

Block was soon appointed to the AAP's Committee on Child Abuse and Neglect (COCAN) and later became its chair. While he was chair in the late 1990s, widespread interest in a new pediatric subspecialty in child abuse burgeoned. Spearheading that movement, Block carried the proposal to the American Board of Pediatrics and the American Board of Medical Specialties, whose approval was required for the creation of a new medical specialty. After the specialty was approved, he became chair of the Sub-Board of Child Abuse Pediatrics. The subboard committee worked diligently to develop a credentials policy and to produce the first certifying exam, which was administered in November 2009. In the same year, Block was named to head the newly formed Academy for Violence and Abuse (See *Chapter 18*).

STEPHEN BOOS, PEDIATRICIAN

Stephen Boos attended medical school in New York at Columbia University and pursued a pediatric residency in the Air Force. There was little or no teaching about child abuse during that time, although he encountered cases. While practicing general pediatrics in the Air Force, Boos encountered more cases (still without instruction), and ultimately, he attended the San Diego Conference on Responding to Child Maltreatment in 1988. There, he met a number of doctors committed to child abuse work, including McCann with whom he completed a fellowship in Fresno, California. Boos became an Air Force child abuse consultant, and when he returned to civilian life, he worked in Montgomery County, Maryland and in New Jersey before becoming the medical director of the Family Advocacy Center at the Baystate Children's Hospital in Springfield, Massachusetts. Along the way, Boos contributed substantially to child abuse literature.

JOCELYN BROWN, PEDIATRICIAN

In 1980, Jocelyn Brown was recruited by Nicholas Cunningham at Columbia University School of Medicine in New York to work in child protection pediatrics at what is now known as the Children's Hospital of New York. Despite Cunningham's considerable prestige, the hospital was reluctant to support a comprehensive child abuse program because of the high costs; however, the doctors invited Matilda Cuomo, the wife of the state governor, to visit and so impressed her with the need for the program that it developed substantial and ongoing support. In addition to her achievements, Brown is fluent in French and contributed substantially to the English translation of Tardieu's writing.

PAT BRUNO, PEDIATRICIAN

In the late 1980s, Pat Bruno was practicing solo general pediatrics in a rural central Pennsylvania setting. Children and Youth Services in his locality brought him child abuse cases, because he was the only available pediatrician. He availed himself of the one-week training program provided by the Center for Child Protection in San Diego and returned to Pennsylvania to develop a more formal program for his area.

One of Bruno's cases involved a 7-year-old girl brought to his clinic after stating that her father sexually abused her. As he prepared to examine her, she asked if he could help heal the "hurt in her heart." For this girl and for others that have followed, Bruno is still trying to answer the question, while continuing to provide a comprehensive service for abused children in his area.

KRISTINE CAMPBELL, PEDIATRICIAN

Figure 13-4

After a pediatric residency, Kristine Campbell **(Figure 13-4)** entered the Indian Health Service (IHS) and served as the pediatrician for the vast, rural central Navajo area child protection team in Arizona. By default, she became the pediatrician for families with a history of abuse and neglect. Finding the work rewarding but frustrating, Campbell could not always distinguish families who would move past a first episode of abuse from those who would repeat the cycle of abuse year after year. She had difficulty understanding how one child with a history of abuse could thrive and succeed while another would be forever damaged by similar abuse.

After 5 years, Campbell left the IHS to pursue research training at the University of Pittsburgh with Berger. Her work there helped her identify practical and effective interventions to improve outcomes for families with a history of abuse. In 2006, she was invited to join the faculty at the University of Utah, where she continues to pursue these career goals.

James Carpenter, Pediatrician

In the early 1980s, James Carpenter completed a pediatric residency at the Children's Hospital of Oakland and took a position at the nearby Contra Costa County Regional Medical Center (CCCRMC), which was in the process of establishing a special service for abused children at a time when blueprints for such services were scarce. Carpenter soon visited the center at Children's Hospital in San Diego and, to some extent, borrowed that model, which provided substantial breadth and depth of the services needed by abused children. Twenty years later, the CCCRMC still provides comprehensive health services for abused children under Carpenter's supervision.

Mary Case, Neuropathologist

Mary Case **(Figure 13-5)** attended medical school at St. Louis University, where she also completed residencies in neuropathology and forensic pathology. In 1977, she became a medical examiner for the city of St. Louis and the surrounding area at the time the jurisdiction transitioned from a coroner to a medical examiner system with pathologists in charge.

Figure 13-5

A medical examiner in a big city is automatically in the path of child abuse cases; however, until the 1970s, many medical examiners failed to recognize them as such. This was not a problem for Case, who immediately recognized many cases of child abuse. A large majority of fatal child abuse cases involve head injuries; therefore, her qualifications in neuropathology were extremely helpful.

Case began her work in an era when there was little writing and little teaching in medical schools about child abuse, but she was able to learn from the cases she saw and to publish her own observations, including the notable position paper of the National Association of Medical Examiners on inflicted head injuries.[6] These publications have placed Case in a leadership position among her peers and among child abuse doctors nationally.

Figure 13-6

DAVID L. CHADWICK, PEDIATRICIAN, THE AUTHOR

David L. Chadwick **(Figure 13-6)** completed his pediatric residency at the University of California, San Francisco (UCSF) in the mid-1950s, when Kempe was an assistant professor there. Chadwick then spent 2 years in fellowships, studying infectious diseases and establishing his career path.

In 1958, he became the director of Outpatient Services for the Children's Hospital of Los Angeles, where he remained for 10 years, and he also became an assistant professor of pediatrics at the University of Southern California (USC). The lone hospital social worker, Helen Boardman, insisted he look at infants who were coming to the hospital repeatedly with multiple fractures and other poorly explained injuries, and the hospital's radiologist, John Gwinn, informed him that some pediatric radiologists suspected these types of fractures were inflicted by a caregiver. Chadwick supported Boardman in the management of the cases seen in Los Angeles, and he testified in both criminal and dependency proceedings in a number of cases.

In 1961, Kempe made a presentation for the AAP titled "The Battered Child Syndrome." Kempe also inquired about cases of this type that were being seen in Los Angeles, and Boardman published an article in the journal *Child Welfare* about child physical abuse in 1962, the same year Kempe's article appeared in the *Journal of the American Medical Association*. In 1962, Kempe invited Boardman and Chadwick to the Children's Bureau conference, where the child abuse reporting law was written. In those years, experience established reporting by doctors would not protect children, unless the doctors also bore witness to the abuse using their medical knowledge.

In 1968, Chadwick became the first medical director of the Children's Hospital in San Diego—an assignment intended to encourage the development of specialized hospital-based medical services there. Child abuse services in San Diego were already relatively advanced. The city police department had a specialized unit for child abuse, and the county Department of Social Services included a worker, Elizabeth Lennon, who was committed to multidisciplinary processes in the evaluation of child abuse cases. A Community Child Abuse Coordinating Council was soon established, and in 1976, the newly established National Center for Child Abuse and Neglect at the US Children's Bureau featured San Diego along with Montgomery County, Maryland and Salina, Kansas as communities with exemplary multidisciplinary teams, filming a video that illustrated the teams at work.

Health services for abused children were developed at the San Diego Children's Hospital throughout the 1970s, and by mid-1980, the chief executive officer, Blair Sadler, and the Board of Trustees authorized the establishment of a hospital department called the Center for Child Protection and appointed Chadwick to become its full-time director. The Center offered a number of services to benefit abused children, including diagnostic and forensic medical services for physical and sexual abuse and neglect; mental health care services for children and families recovering from abuse; and preventive services in the form of home-visiting programs that provided support to families in distress. In 1986, the first San Diego Conference on Responding to Child Maltreatment was held. About 100 doctors attended, but the conference was later made multidisciplinary and, now, attracts up to 2000 professionals annually.

Chadwick retired from the Children's Hospital in 1997 and worked, for a time, as a consultant. From 2002 to 2004, he worked part-time at the University of Utah Department of Pediatrics as a researcher. Over the years, he has made a number of contributions to the medical literature on child abuse.

DAVID CORWIN

David Corwin's **(Figure 13-7)** first contact with the problem of child abuse came from Helfer, because he was one of 2 faculty preceptors during Corwin's first 10 weeks of medical school at Michigan State College of Human Medicine in 1972. He encountered several cases of child abuse and incest during his residency in psychiatry at the Sepulveda VA Medical Center, but his primary mentor in child sexual abuse was Roland Summit during his child psychiatric fellowship at the University of California, Los Angeles (UCLA).

Figure 13-7

After Corwin's training was complete and he became board-certified in child psychiatry in 1982, he opened a private practice of child, adolescent, and adult psychiatry in Orinda, California. As one of the first child psychiatrists trained in depth about child sexual abuse, he immediately began to offer videotaped interviews of children suspected of being abused along with his analyses for testimony in litigated cases. While still a child psychiatry fellow at UCLA, Corwin assembled and chaired the Los Angeles Task Force on Interviewing Sexually Abused Children. That group was the first to present and advocate the video recording of investigative interviews with children in suspected child sexual abuse cases both at a national conference in the US and the Fourth International Congress on Child Abuse and Neglect in Paris in 1982.

Corwin quickly became acquainted with other professionals working in this new field and organized a major meeting in Los Angeles, using his own resources and gathering many of the leaders of the new field of child abuse. He dubbed this conference the "National Summit Conference on Diagnosing Child Sexual Abuse" (a deliberate pun), and it led to the creation of the California Professional Society on the Abuse of Children (CAPSAC). Soon thereafter, at a meeting in New Orleans organized by pioneering nurse Joyce Thomas, the idea of a similar multidisciplinary national society took hold, and it resulted in the founding of the American Professional Society on the Abuse of Children (APSAC). Corwin was a prime mover, chairing the group that founded APSAC.

As a leading advocate for greater participation of the health care system, including personal and public health, in the child abuse picture, Corwin has lobbied for change with the American Academy of Child and Adolescent Psychiatry (AACAP); the AAP's COCAN; the American Medical Association's National Advisory Council on Violence and Abuse; and the more recently formed Academy on Violence and Abuse. He has carried that battle to Washington, where the idea has received favorable attention. Corwin's publications deal with major issues, such as the cycles of suppression of child abuse knowledge and forensic psychiatric aspects of the problem.

KEVIN COULTER, PEDIATRICIAN
In 1982, Kevin Coulter was practicing general pediatrics at the San Francisco General Hospital, a major teaching facility for the UCSF School of Medicine. The senior pediatrician, Moses Grossman urged Coulter to establish a service for abused children because many were being seen in the large county hospital. Coulter began providing consultations for both physically and sexually abused children. In the sexual abuse program, he was assisted by obstetrician Bonnie Dattell.

About 20 years later in 2001, Coulter migrated to the Sacramento Medical Center at the University of California, Davis where he still practices child abuse medicine and provides comprehensive services to abused children in that region.

THEODORE CURPHEY, PATHOLOGIST
Theodore Curphey was the first pathologist to work as a medical examiner in Los Angeles County. He wrote the first article about child abuse published by a pathologist since the writings of Tardieu a century earlier. Despite publishing just one article in a state medical journal,[7] Curphey was so far ahead of his peers that he deserves a special mention.

MORE STORIES
The next chapter will describe more of the doctors who were "early adopters" in this field.

REFERENCES

1. Flaherty EG, et al. Health care providers' experience reporting child abuse in the primary care setting. Pediatric Practice Research Group. *Arch Pediatr Adolesc Med.* 2000;154(5):489-493.

2. Adams J. The Wake-up Call. *West J Med.* 1993;159(4):514-515.

3. Helfer RE, et al. Trauma to the bones of small infants from passive exercise: a factor in the etiology of child abuse. *J Pediatr.* 1984;104(1):47-50.

4. Anderson SB. Sexual Assault. In: Eisenberg M, Copass M, eds. *Emergency Medical Therapy.* Philadelphia, PA: Saunders; 1982:292-293.

5. Berger RP, Kochanek PM, Pierce MC. Biochemical markers of brain injury: could they be used as diagnostic adjuncts in cases of inflicted traumatic brain injury? *Child Abuse Negl.* 2004; 28(7):739-754.

6. Case ME, et al. Position paper on fatal abusive head injuries in infants and young children. *Am J Forensic Med Pathol.* 2001;22(2):112-122.

7. Curphey TJ, et al. The Battered Child Syndrome. Responsibilities of the Pathologist. *Calif Med.* 1965;02:102-104.

Chapter 14

Doctors' Stories: D-I

We few, we happy few, we band of brothers;
For he to-day that sheds his blood with me
Shall be my brother…

— **William Shakespeare**, from *Henry V*

This chapter adds more stories of doctors who were "early adopters" of child abuse medicine.

Doctors' Stories (continued)

The following entries are arranged in alphabetical order; therefore, the order of these doctors' stories is not an indicator of importance.

Mark Dias, Pediatric Neurosurgeon

An undergraduate excursion into a neurobiology laboratory stimulated Mark Dias to become involved with the brain and become a medical doctor, ultimately traveling the long road to pediatric neurosurgery. At the Children's Hospital in Buffalo in 1997, he encountered infants with inflicted brain injuries at the same time his own child was born. He became fascinated with the problems connected to abusive head trauma and began to do research and publish articles on the subject.

Reasoning that many cases of abusive head trauma might be prevented if new parents were aware of the dangers of certain actions, especially shaking infants, Dias obtained funding from the state of New York to initiate an educational program designed to prevent this form of abuse. Although statistical proof that abusive head trauma is being prevented requires studies of large popu-lations, the results are encouraging enough that this educational approach, targeting new parents, is likely to become widespread. A national authority on the mechanisms of abusive head trauma, Dias is rightly regarded as a leader in the field of prevention of shaken baby syndrome.

Howard Dubowitz, Pediatrician

Howard Dubowitz (**Figure 14-1**) was born and brought up in South Africa and started his medical career in London as a family physician. He migrated to Boston Children's Hospital for a residency

Figure 14-1

in pediatrics and learned about child abuse in that setting, eventually emerging as a fully trained child abuse pediatrician in 1981.

He has built a well-recognized program at the University of Maryland and contributed substantially to the field with an emphasis on the problems produced by child neglect and the methods of child maltreatment prevention. In 2009, Dubowitz published encouraging results of a simple and inexpensive child maltreatment prevention program that could be provided easily in any children's primary health care setting.[1]

ANN CHRISTIAN DUHAIME, PEDIATRIC NEUROSURGEON

Ann Christian Duhaime became a pediatric neurosurgeon by completing a residency at the Children's Hospital of Philadelphia in the early 1980s at a time when Stephen Ludwig had already established a child protection team at that hospital. Criteria for the recognition of physically abused children, including those with head injuries, were already in place; however, because the histories of abused children were almost invariably incorrect, there was still a lot to be learned about head injury mechanisms. Also, at that time, the University of Pennsylvania was at the forefront of biomechanical research about head injuries because of the work of Thomas Genneralli, Susan Margulies, and others. Duhaime quickly recognized that inflicted head injuries in abused children comprised a large part of the work of neurosurgeons in her hospital.

With a large caseload of children with head injuries of both unintentional and inflicted natures and with excellent research facilities and a strong research environment, Duhaime was perfectly positioned to study and analyze inflicted head injury problems. This work was inherently controversial; cases of inflicted head injuries frequently led to adversarial criminal proceedings, affecting the children's caregivers. Previous knowledge of injury mechanisms in such cases had come from confessions by caregivers recorded by Norman Guthkelch and John Caffey, who had defined shaken baby syndrome to explain serious head injuries in infants without apparent external head injury. It became important to attempt to determine if serious and fatal head injuries in infants could be produced by shaking. In 1987,[2] Duhaime published data showing that impact of the rapidly moving head produced much greater force than shaking alone. This did not produce a final answer to the question concerning the effects of shaking, but was interpreted irresponsibly to indicate that shaking could not cause serious brain damage. Duhaime is one of the most important contributors to knowledge about inflicted head injuries and their importance in the overall picture of child abuse.

KATHLEEN DULLY, PEDIATRICIAN

While an intern at the US Naval Hospital in Oakland, Kathleen Dully **(Figure 14-2)** encountered her first case of abusive head trauma in an infant, which was immediately followed by the denial by a fellow resident, who found it impossible to believe that a mother might injure her baby. Later, at the US Naval Hospital in Jacksonville, Florida, Dully was arbitrarily assigned to a child abuse team and was able to obtain training in San Diego at the San Diego Conference and in a fellowship at what was then called the Center for Child Protection at the San Diego Children's Hospital. She was then assigned to the San Diego area by the Navy and organized an effective area-wide multidisciplinary child abuse program, involving 2 Naval hospitals and a number of outpatient clinics in the area. This work was interrupted when she was reassigned to provide care to injured Marines in Iraq, and the Navy was unable to sustain the multidisciplinary program she had built in the San Diego area. Dully retired from the Navy and still practices child abuse pediatrics at the Chadwick Center for Children and Families at the Rady Children's Hospital in San Diego.

Figure 14-2

MICHAEL DURFEE, PUBLIC HEALTH PSYCHIATRIST

Michael Durfee **(Figure 14-3)** was educated as a psychiatrist; however, he has done more to bring a public health approach to the field of child abuse medicine than most public health professionals, including several surgeons-general. Durfee received an experiential education in child abuse when, shortly after completing a psychiatric residency, he was assigned to provide care to children admitted to Los Angeles County's emergency shelter. At that time in the 1970s, the older children in the dependency system were often heavily medicated, and Durfee cut medications and increased listening and thus learned about child abuse.

Figure 14-3

Also, many doctors working with abused children were busy developing centers, which could provide in-depth care, but Durfee took a somewhat different tack and attempted to ensure every hospital with an emergency department, where children might be seen, had a doctor and a social worker competent about child abuse. This approach provided the maximum number of children with quick access to a respectable—if not perfect—level of care. Durfee was quite successful in his endeavor, increasing the number of hospitals in Los Angeles County with child abuse teams from 6 to 35 over about a 5-year period around 1980.

In addition to those great achievements, Durfee is best known for inventing and disseminating the practice of multidisciplinary child death review, a system that casts a broad net and looks at child deaths of all kinds and attempts to sort out those deaths that need a more intensive investigation for child abuse and those that were otherwise preventable. His missionary work with this concept resulted in the development of child death review teams in almost every state, with either state or local support. This is a public health approach to child abuse and will ultimately lead to effective ways of measuring the most severe health harms of abuse. Reliable measurement is the first public health step toward prevention.

NORMAN S. ELLERSTEIN, PEDIATRICIAN

In the mid-1970s, Norman Ellerstein launched a child abuse program at the Children's Hospital of Buffalo and the State University of New York, Department of Pediatrics. His work there and his example inspired Betty Spivack and Jack Coyne, among others, to become involved in child abuse medical work.

Ellerstein was a pioneer in many ways; he called attention to the sexual abuse of boys at a time when almost all published work on the subject emphasized the predominance of female victims. Best known for his 1981 edited book, which concentrated on the medical aspects of child abuse, Ellerstein provided practical guidelines for doctors of the time to deal with child abuse cases, as they presented themselves in medical settings.[3]

His work and his life were interrupted by illness, but he made major contributions. Speaking at the time of Ellerstein's death at age 41, T. Dennis Sullivan, one of his close associates, said of his work in child abuse, "That's a field that has very little glitter and very little gold." If there has been a growth of the value and recognition of child abuse medicine, Ellerstein can be credited for much of it.

V. DENISE EVERETT, PEDIATRICIAN

V. Denise Everett started her pediatric career in a mixture of private practice and general pediatrics in a public health clinic. She was soon recruited to the Wake Medical Center in Raleigh, North Carolina by David Ingram for the express purpose of establishing a clinic for sexually abused children. Very early in the history of that program, one of her associates was sexually assaulted and murdered on the Wake Medical campus. The violent act so close to home solidified Everett's resolve to pursue child abuse work. Directing and operating the child abuse program soon became a full-time position, and she has continued her work up to the time of this writing. Despite the limited funding typical of hospital-based child abuse programs, Everett has made substantial contributions to knowledge in the field.

KENNETH FELDMAN, PEDIATRICIAN

While practicing general pediatrics in Seattle, Kenneth Feldman published an article in 1978 about tap water burns, including a number that were not accidental. The article caught the attention of Ray E. Helfer, who asked Feldman to write a chapter on inflicted burns for a new (5th) edition of the textbook *The Battered Child*. Feldman then became the principal child abuse consultant for the Children's Orthopedic Hospital in Seattle and for the Harborview Medical Center. An expert in all forms of child maltreatment, Feldman published a number of articles over the ensuing years.

Feldman has also encountered a substantial cluster of cases of the condition then known as Munchausen syndrome by proxy, which resulted in his being extensively harassed by persons involved with that issue and, to some extent, by local media. Surviving this onslaught, he has continued to gain national visibility for his insightful descriptions of various forms of child maltreatment.

VINCENT FELITTI, INTERNIST
Vincent Felitti became involved in child abuse by accident, having had no prior interest in the subject. Formerly an internist doing infectious disease work, he had set up a department of preventive medicine in which he was operating an obesity program, using the technique of supplemented absolute fasting for patients who were dangerously obese, a method that produced rapid and dramatic results. Counter-intuitively, Felitti discovered that such success was enormously threatening to patients, who either fled or quickly regained the lost weight. He soon discovered that many of the patients had been sexually abused as children and were unconsciously using obesity as a way of protectively de-sexing themselves. Being overweight was not the patients' problem, it was their solution, and taking their solution away was enormously threatening.

As Felitti pursued this discovery further, he discovered how common other forms of child abuse and dysfunctional households were. By adult life, this was all buried in time and further protected by shame, secrecy, and social taboos against exploring certain areas of human experience. These clinical observations led the Adverse Childhood Experiences (ACE) study to explore the prevalence and impact in a general population of such adverse childhood experiences decades later. The ACE study was carried out in a very large middle class population of persons subscribing to the Kaiser Permanente System that largely serves employed groups and not persons in poverty.

Ultimately, Felitti came to see that "adverse childhood experiences" were the main engine underlying some of our most serious public health problems: obesity, alcoholism, intractable smoking, drug use, depression, promiscuity, and secondary conditions like diabetes, certain cancers, and heart disease. Felitti's work establishes that enormous gains in the public health and savings in health costs could be achieved if child abuse and other forms of adverse experiences can be reduced by prevention. The ACE study has given birth to about 40 reviewed publications, and a few of the most important ones are cited.[4-10]

MARTIN A. FINKEL, PEDIATRICIAN

Figure 14-4

In his pediatric residency at Columbus Children's Hospital, Martin A. Finkel **(Figure 14-4)** learned about physical abuse, but sexual abuse was not mentioned. In 1981, he was asked to attend a lecture on the subject given by Suzanne Sgroi, the Connecticut pioneer, and was shocked to learn about the severity of the problem. Returning to his faculty position at the School of Osteopathic Medicine at the University of Medicine and Dentistry of New Jersey, Finkel was determined to do something about child sexual abuse. He began to speak about child sexual abuse and encountered physicians and other professionals who had never seen it despite many years in practice. This was a phenomenon that he recognized as "simple blindness to abuse," a widespread ocular affliction of medical doctors.

Most of Finkel's publications describe work with sexual abuse, and they include landmark work on the healing of genital injuries and a definitive manual for medical evaluation[11]; however, he is also widely recognized for persuading a large state government apparatus to support medical services for abused children so that such services are easily accessible to all or most children in the state of New Jersey. Only Florida has a more accessible and competent statewide health-based system.

EMALEE FLAHERTY, PEDIATRICIAN

For many years, Emalee Flaherty provided medical services for abused children at the Children's Memorial Hospital in Chicago and the Department of Pediatrics of Northwestern University School of Medicine. Her publications cover a wide variety of issues in child abuse, especially the issue of doctors' reporting behaviors. She observed that doctors report abuse inconsistently and that this problem has been fed from difficulties in understanding such legal terms as "reasonable suspicion" and "other than accidental." She also noted that relationships between doctors and the parents of patients interfere with reporting.

VINCENT FONTANA, A PEDIATRIC PIONEER IN NEW YORK CITY

Vincent Fontana's association, in the 1960s, with the New York Foundling Hospital, a facility for abandoned infants established by the Catholic Order of St. Vincent De Paul a century earlier, placed him in the path of many neglected and abused children. Soon after

C. Henry Kempe's breakthrough article, Fontana published, in 1963[12] and in 1964,[13] about his own experiences, which were similar to Kempe's, although colored by New York's comparatively violent environment. Writing about abandonment in his city, Fontana noted: "Indeed as late as 1892, 200 foundlings and 100 dead infants were found in New York City streets." He described injuries similar to those depicted by Kempe and emphasized that physical abuse was part of a continuum of maltreatment connected to neglect. He emphasized the importance of doctors' testimony in litigated cases.

Fontana recognized the importance of poverty and other social factors to the causation of physical abuse and neglect of children. He labored throughout his long career to help the families of children in New York avoid abuse and neglect. Active in New York City politics, he made child abuse an important local issue and published extensively in medical journals. His popular book, *Somewhere A Child Is Crying*, describes the important features of child mal-treatment in plain language and also describes efforts to deal with the problem at both individual and institutional levels. Many of Fontana's observations and recommendations are still valid 30 years later; however, the systemic problems that limit effectiveness of intervention and prevention persist in New York, as they have throughout the US.

GILLES FORTIN, PEDIATRICIAN

Gilles Fortin first learned about child abuse from a lecture by Helfer given in Montreal in 1971 to an audience of incredulous pediatricians—some of whom believed that child abuse would not happen in the religiously devout, well-behaved population of Montreal. Following that lecture and an increased level of pediatric consciousness, child abuse cases began to be recognized there, and a special clinic was established.

In 1987, Fortin joined the health department in Montreal and became involved in child abuse work on a full-time basis. Because he was fluent in French, he was able to assist in the English translation of the work of Auguste Ambroise Tardieu. He also published work about neurological problems arising from child abuse.

LORI FRASIER, PEDIATRICIAN

Lori Frasier (**Figure 14-5**) completed a pediatric residency at Harborview Hospital in Seattle in 1986 and came to know Carole Jenny, who steered her toward an interest in child abuse, and after her residency, Frasier spent a year in a child abuse fellowship. Frasier then moved to the University of Iowa and became acquainted with Randell Alexander, who was heading the child abuse program there

Figure 14-5

at that time. In addition to diagnostic services for physical and sexual abuse, the program at Iowa included a Family Assessment Clinic based on a developmental disabilities model that allowed thorough and detailed family assessments, providing valuable insights into the ways in which maltreatment occurs.

After moving to the University of Missouri in Columbia, Frasier became the head of General Pediatrics in that medical school and directed a program for child abuse as well. She became increasingly involved at the national level and was elected to chair the Section on Child Abuse and Neglect (SOCAN) of the American Academy of Pediatrics (AAP). She was also able to train fellows at the University of Missouri. In 2001, Frasier moved to her hometown of Salt Lake City, Utah and joined the faculty at the University of Utah and the Primary Children's Hospital. Having published extensively about all aspects of child maltreatment in journals, Frasier has also edited a major reference text on children's inflicted injuries.[14]

JILL GLICK, PEDIATRICIAN

Jill Glick completed her pediatric residency at the University of Chicago Comer Children's Hospital around 1985 and immediately plunged into the reorganization of the pediatric emergency department for the busy Children's Hospital. Cases of both physical and sexual abuse were coming to the emergency department in large numbers, and Glick organized services to deal with child abuse more effectively. Although she was given substantial support by the Children's Hospital's administrative structure, the academic component from the University of Chicago School of Medicine did nothing to encourage the development of child abuse services. In fact, a committee of the School informed her that working on child abuse was "an academic dead-end." This was a fairly common attitude in medical schools in the 1980s.

Glick was influenced and assisted by a number of Chicago doctors who were pioneering the child abuse field, including the crusading pathologist Robert Kirschner and child abuse pediatricians in other major Chicago hospitals, Demetra Soter, Michele Lorand, and Flaherty. She was further motivated by the tragic nature of many of the cases that came to her attention in the early years of program development.

In about a decade, Glick was able to construct a complete child abuse medical program at the Comer Children's Hospital. Together with other Chicago child abuse doctors and the public social services and law enforcement agencies, she built a comprehensive response system for child abuse cases involving all the necessary disciplines and authorities. In a multi-year commitment to an interdisciplinary task force composed of physicians and other representatives from child welfare, judicial, and criminal professions, the State of Illinois awarded $1 million each year to create a model system for the investigation of child abuse. The Multidisciplinary Pediatric Education and Evaluation Consortium (MPEEC) has provided a statewide network of physicians skilled in and dedicated to the detection, diagnosis, and legal follow-up of abuse and has made this expertise readily available to hospitals and child protective services throughout Illinois. Glick's clinical and organizational work left little time for research or publication, but she has still made a significant contribution.[15]

Jane Gray, Pediatrician

Jane Gray was associated with Kempe in the early days of the Kempe Center in Denver, Colorado. Together with Kempe and 2 other workers, she conducted the first study that demonstrated the feasibility of predicting child abuse risk and the effectiveness of interventions, which consist simply of heightened attention by primary pediatric care providers.[16] As of this book's writing, Gray is still a contributing child abuse doctor at the Kempe Center.

Frederick Green, Pediatrician

Frederick Green initiated the child abuse program at the Children's Hospital National Medical Center in Washington, DC in the early to mid-1970s (see *Chapter 4*). He published just a few articles, but he was extremely influential in moving health care professionals into the child abuse field.

Elisabeth Guenther, Pediatrician

Elisabeth Guenther, an associate professor at the University of Utah School of Medicine, is board-certified in pediatrics and pediatric emergency medicine. She had special research interest in the presentation and diagnosis of child abuse in the emergency department setting and garnered funding in this area from the National Institute of Child Health and Development (NICHD). Her research has resulted in several publications.[17,18] She also contributed to a chapter on falls in the 2010 textbook by Jenny titled *Child Abuse and Neglect: Diagnosis, Treatment, and Evidence*.

Astrid Heger, Pediatrician

Astrid Heger received instruction from Shirley Anderson in the 1970s in Seattle and began to provide service in Los Angeles just in time to perform medical examinations on a number of the children involved in the McMartin Day Care Center Case (see *Chapter 8*). This case, especially, exemplified the defense tactic of personal attacks launched in the media against professionals acting as witnesses for children. In 1986, Heger had collaborated with Bruce Woodling to publish a description of the use of colposcopic examination to detect genital injuries in child abuse victims.[19] This work became important in the McMartin case. Shortly afterward, the technique was challenged in another litigated case and upheld by a California court of appeals. As of 2010, Heger continues to provide services to abused children and has contributed many useful observations to the literature.

RAY E. HELFER, PEDIATRICIAN

Figure 14-6

Helfer **(Figure 14-6)** often spoke about his early association with Kempe in the mid-1960s and how the first edition of their book, *The Battered Child*, was written. Kempe had presented the idea to the University of Chicago Press, and it had been accepted in principle. He then shared with Helfer his thoughts about the chapter topics and possible authors, but at that point, Kempe went to India to continue work on a smallpox vaccine, a project that occupied much of his time. Handing his notes and the letter from the University of Chicago Press to Helfer, Kempe said, "Take care of this, Ray" and left to catch an airplane. When he returned months later, the writing of the book was well under way, and Helfer became the senior editor. The authors included medical doctors, social workers, sociologists, lawyers, law enforcement officers, and a pediatric medical historian. The book set the multidisciplinary tone that has characterized the field ever since, although, sadly, the historian failed to emphasize the important 19th-century contributions of Tardieu.

A few years later, Helfer left Colorado to take a position in New York and soon moved on to Michigan State University in East Lansing. He continued to study child maltreatment and to speak and write extensively on the subject. He always searched for ways in which health care professionals could contribute to the amelioration of child abuse and its harmful effects. He firmly believed in mandated reporting by doctors, but decried criminal prosecution, believing better methods for prevention could be discovered. While still in Colorado, he developed an interest in the processes of attachment of mothers and children, which led to his publication of the humane and insightful book, *Childhood Comes First*.[20] The book is written for adults who themselves were abused or neglected in childhood and explains how they may compensate later in life by learning the skills of attachment and parenting after becoming parents themselves.

Helfer was interested in the naming of different child maltreatment forms and particularly the way in which names influenced thinking about the problems. In the 1980s, injury researchers in the US proposed dividing all injuries into 2 classes, "unintentional" and "intentional," eliminating the adjective "accidental," with its implication of inevitability. Because of the difficulty in determining parents' or caregivers' intent, Helfer strenuously objected to the term "intentional injury" to describe injuries seen in abused children. In many cases, he realized that parents did not intend to kill or maim their children, but they used violent methods of control and produced damage they did not predict or plan. Helfer's influence was great, and doctors working in the field of child abuse medicine still avoid the term "intentional injury," using "non-accidental trauma" (NAT) instead, although *some* sort of intent must be present in most cases of serious abuse.

Helfer's extensive writing and speaking were important in the development of child abuse medicine. To him, an orientation toward prevention was more important than forensic proof and criminal sanctions. Still, his observations of children's short falls occurring in hospitals[21] provided an important forensic medical contribution that has been useful in the prosecution of criminal cases. Helfer also originated the idea of Children's Trust Funds. These are funds, built on donations by taxpayers at the state level, that are used for family support and child abuse prevention programs administered by states. The idea has spread to many states and continues to grow.

Helfer died of a stroke at the early age of 62. He was working on observations of the parenting behaviors of captive primates at the time of his death. Helfer's death interrupted a career that was leading toward the prevention of child abuse by health professionals.

Bruce Herman, Pediatrician

In the spring of 1997, Bruce Herman, a pediatric emergency physician, was working in the primary Children's Hospital in Salt Lake City, Utah and the Department of Pediatrics in the University of Utah School of Medicine when W. Martin Palmer died unexpectedly. Palmer had been providing services for abused children almost single-handedly, and Herman took over the program without much preparation. However, he was able to attend conferences and to form consulting relationships and was soon engulfed in a growing medical program that included Karen Hansen, Guenther, Frasier, and David Corwin. Herman has helped to build the Salt Lake City program into a national model.

Judith L. Herman, Psychiatrist

Judith L. Herman, a psychiatrist at Harvard University, provided a new depth of understanding of posttraumatic stress disorder in her landmark book published in 1997, titled *Trauma and Recovery*.[22] In this book, she describes the serious complex of symptoms experienced by soldiers after combat, by captives (such as prisoners of war and political prisoners), and by victims of child abuse and some natural disasters that all led to a common pathway. Illuminating this new branch of psychology, Herman coined the name, complex posttraumatic stress disorder, to describe the specific manifestations brought about by prolonged abusive experiences. Herman's numerous published articles deal with many of the most important issues in child maltreatment, with a particular focus on sexual abuse, its origins, its effects, and the sad history of the early psychiatric response.

ROBERTA HIBBARD, PEDIATRICIAN

Roberta Hibbard encountered her first child abuse case while an intern, and was required to testify in the criminal trial that followed. No one should be asked to perform this difficult procedure for the first time without support and guidance. Later, when her knowledge of child abuse was more advanced, her mother, a kindergarten teacher, brought her a bizarre drawing made by a pre-kindergartner as part of school readiness screening. There were disconnected eyes, arms, legs, a hairy chest, and a "wiener." The drawing was of the child's father. No one knew if the presence of private parts in the picture meant anything, so Hibbard obtained very strong (and contradictory) opinions from nationally prominent pediatricians on the drawing. When the child in question started kindergarten in the fall, Hibbard asked her mother to follow up on the student's case. She learned the child had disclosed 2 weeks before school that she was being molested. This launched Hibbard's interest in children's drawings and a series of studies that elucidated the value of this method for diagnosing children who had been sexually abused.

After joining the faculty at Indiana University, Hibbard was based at the Riley Children's Hospital in Indianapolis, where she has built a comprehensive medical child abuse program that serves the entire state of Indiana. In the process, she has been able to convince the state social services sector that they do, indeed, require medical doctors to evaluate most children suspected of being abused. Hibbard has published extensively on a variety of child abuse issues.

SUSAN HOROWITZ, FAMILY DOCTOR

After attending medical school and completing an internship in New York City, Susan Horowitz migrated to San Diego and the family medicine program at the University of California, San Diego (UCSD) School of Medicine. She worked in the student health offices at UCSD, where she encountered physicians who were providing services for suspected sexual abuse victims at the

Children's Hospital's Center for Child Protection. After being recruited to help out in that program, she began to treat sexually abused children.

Because of her orientation in a consciousness-raising group, decades earlier, that dealt with women's issues, Horowitz was better prepared than most doctors to deal with the problem. She brought with her the theories of the women's movement, which facilitated acceptance of the hard facts of child sexual abuse. She became involved at a time when the use of magnified examinations of the genitalia was just beginning, and the details of normal genital anatomy of children were still being defined.

Twenty-five years later, Horowitz is still providing medical evaluations of children suspected of being sexually abused. She has published about a sexually transmitted disease and the occurrence of sexual abuse.[23]

MARK HORTON, PUBLIC HEALTH PRACTITIONER

Mark Horton learned about child abuse from patients, while providing care to the high-risk population at Boys' Town in Nebraska. He then worked for 2 years as the director for the Center for Child Protection at the Children's Hospital in San Diego before becoming the director of the newly formed Department of Public Health in California. Horton is one of the few state health officers who is well informed and experienced with child abuse.

KENT HYMEL, PEDIATRICIAN

Kent Hymel **(Figure 14-7)** was serving in the US Air Force at Keesler Air Force Base in one of a very few Air Force teaching hospitals, and he was in charge of ambulatory care and pediatric education. One day in 1989, his commanding officer stopped him in the hallway and asked him to start a child abuse program. Hymel's protests that he had no prior experience with this work were unavailing, and military discipline prevailed, thus altering his career forever. After some successful work in the field, he was able to persuade the Air Force to send him to Denver for a fellowship in child abuse pediatrics under the tutelage of Jenny. He became the first US Air Force consultant to the Surgeon General in child abuse and neglect.

Figure 14-7

After completing his military obligation, Hymel migrated to the University of Virginia and thence to the Dartmouth-Hitchcock Medical Center in New Hampshire. He has made many original contributions and may be most notable for an effort to connect child abuse medicine to biomechanical engineering in order to improve understanding of head injury mechanisms and the differentiation of unintentional from intentional head injuries.

MORE STORIES

Child abuse doctors have often encountered skepticism, indifference, and sometimes opposition in pursuing their important work. As the next chapter will show, these problems persist.

REFERENCES

1. Dubowitz H, et al. Pediatric primary care to help prevent child maltreatment: the Safe Environment for Every Kid (SEEK) model. *Pediatr.* 2009;123(3):858-864.

2. Duhaime AC, et al. The shaken baby syndrome. A clinical, pathological, and biomechanical study. *J Neurosurg.* 1987;66(3):409-415.

3. Ellerstein NS, ed. *Child Abuse and Neglect: A Medical Reference.* New York, NY: John Wiley & Sons; 1981.

4. Anda RF, et al. Adverse childhood experiences and prescription drug use in a cohort study of adult HMO patients. *BMC Public Health.* 2008;8:198.

5. Anda RF, et al. Adverse childhood experiences and risk of paternity in teen pregnancy. *Obstet Gynecol.* 2002;100(1):37-45.

6. Anda RF, et al. Adverse childhood experiences, alcoholic parents, and later risk of alcoholism and depression. *Psychiatr Serv.* 2002;53(8):1001-1009.

7. Dube SR, et al. Adverse childhood experiences and personal alcohol abuse as an adult. *Addict Behav.* 2002;27(5):713-725.

8. Dube SR, et al. Assessing the reliability of retrospective reports of adverse childhood experiences among adult HMO members attending a primary care clinic. *Child Abuse Negl.* 2004;28(7):729-737.

9. Felitti VJ, et al. Relationship of childhood abuse and household dysfunction to many of the leading causes of death in adults. The Adverse Childhood Experiences (ACE) Study [see comments]. *Am J Prev Med.* 1998;14(4):245-258.

10. Hillis SD, et al. Adverse childhood experiences and sexually transmitted diseases in men and women: a retrospective study. *Pediatr.* 2000;106(1):E11.

11. Finkel MA. Technical conduct of the child sexual abuse medical examination. *Child Abuse Negl.* 1998;22(6):555-566.

12. Fontana VJ, Donovan D, Wong RJ. The "Maltreatment Syndrome" in Children. *N Engl J Med.* 1963;269:1389-1394.

13. Fontana VJ. The Neglect and Abuse of Children. *N Y State J Med*. 1964;64:215-224.

14. Frasier L, Parrish R, eds. *Abusive Head Trauma in Infants and Children: A Medical, Legal, and Forensic Reference*. St. Louis, MO: G.W. Medical Pub; 2006.

15. Glick JC, Staley K. Inflicted traumatic brain injury: advances in evaluation and collaborative diagnosis. *Pediatr Neurosurg*. 2007;43(5):436-441.

16. Gray JO, et al. Prediction and prevention of child abuse and neglect. *Child Abuse Negl*. 1977;1(1):45-58.

17. Guenther E, et al. Prediction of child abuse risk from emergency department use. *J Pediatr*. 2009;154(2):272-277.

18. Guenther E, et al. Randomized prospective study to evaluate child abuse documentation in the emergency department. *Acad Emerg Med*. 2009;16(3):249-257.

19. Woodling BA, Heger A. The use of the colposcope in the diagnosis of sexual abuse in the pediatric age group. *Child Abuse Negl*. 1986;10(1):111-114.

20. Helfer RE. *Childhood Comes First: A Crash Course in Childhood for Adults*. Self-published; 1984.

21. Helfer RE, Slovis TL, Black M. Injuries resulting when small children fall out of bed. *Pediatr*. 1977;60(4):533-535.

22. Herman JL. *Trauma and Recovery: The Aftermath of Violence— From Domestic Abuse to Political Terror*. New York, NY: Basic Books; 1997:7-14.

23. Horowitz S, Chadwick DL. Syphilis as a sole indicator of sexual abuse: two cases with no intervention. *Child Abuse Negl*. 1990; 14(1):129-132.

Chapter 15

Doctors' Stories: J-O

Sweet are the uses of adversity....

— **William Shakespeare**, from *As You Like It*

The stories of child abuse doctors illustrate the wide variety of pathways that doctors have followed to concentrate on this work. This chapter describes more of these stories and the difficulties doctors encountered as a new medical specialty emerged.

Doctors' Stories (continued)

The following entries are arranged in alphabetical order, and the order of these doctors' stories is not an indicator of importance.

Carole Jenny, Pediatrician

Carole Jenny (**Figure 15-1**) began her career in child abuse medicine at Harborview Hospital in Seattle under the tutelage of Shirley Anderson. In this process, she quickly legitimized the development of the new specialty as a component of academic medicine. A few years later, she migrated to Denver where she assisted the ongoing development of the Kempe National Center and trained a number of fellows. By that time, she had acquired clinical and research skills for all forms of child maltreatment.

Figure 15-1

After moving on to start a new program at Brown University School of Medicine and the Hasbro Children's Hospital in Providence, Jenny carried out important research in all aspects of child maltreatment, publishing extensively on her findings. She inspired many pediatricians to specialize in child abuse, and her edited book on medical evidence in child abuse[1] provides guidance to doctors and lawyers dealing with litigated cases. As talk of formally recognizing the new pediatric subspecialty for child abuse took place in the 1990s, Jenny contributed mightily to the definition of the discipline and the design of graduate medical curricula for doctors who wish to follow this pathway.

Charles Johnson, Pediatrician

Charles Johnson completed a pediatric residency at the Children's Hospital of Los Angeles not long after Helen Boardman had established a policy and procedure there for the reporting of suspected nonaccidental injuries to law enforcement and the local county child protective services. He saw his first case of physical abuse in that setting and was able to obtain an admission of an inflicted burn by the child's mother, which he duly reported. After completing a fellowship in child development in the same setting, he was required to serve in the Army for 2 years.

While assigned to a hospital in Nuremberg, Germany, Johnson dealt with a case involving an infant with a life-threatening head injury and learned that the baby's mother had thrown the baby against a wall. The Army had no procedure for dealing with such a case in a foreign country, and Johnson's attempts to develop an intervention resulted in his transfer from a base hospital to a tank battalion aid station; however, the infant and the parents were returned to the US to an Army base that had a procedure for child abuse in place.

After service in the Army, Johnson moved to the University of Iowa and pursued a career in developmental pediatrics—a specialty that requires a multidisciplinary approach to cases in a manner similar to that needed for child abuse; therefore, child abuse cases were referred to the developmental pediatric team, and its members began to acquire skill. From Iowa, he moved to a new medical school in East Tennessee where he found all forms of child maltreatment prevalent in the surrounding community, and he began to pursue this specialty on a full-time basis. When a full-time position in child abuse pediatrics became available at the Columbus Children's Hospital, Johnson moved there and continued child abuse work until his retirement in 2006. He made many contributions to the field in the form of reviewed articles. In addition to all his achievements in medicine, Johnson is a talented artist. For a number of years, his ingenious cartoons brightened the newsletter, *SCAN*, which he wrote and edited for the American Academy of Pediatrics' (AAP) Section on Child Abuse and Neglect (SOCAN).

RICHARD KAPLAN, PEDIATRICIAN

An undergraduate in Ohio in 1970, Richard Kaplan was in jail following the Kent State Massacre when he realized that he wanted to make a difference in the lives of children and that working with children might give important meaning to his own life.

Kaplan obtained a master's degree in social work and became a mental health therapist. He treated children and soon heard many histories of child sexual abuse. After medical school, he had a pediatric residency in Phoenix and was taught to do medical examinations for sexually abused children at the Maricopa County Hospital. Thus, he was exceptionally well equipped to establish a child abuse program when he took a faculty position at the University of South Dakota in 1996. In 2008, he moved on to the Midwest Children's Resource Center in St. Paul, Minnesota and the University of Minnesota.

SANDRA KAPLAN, PSYCHIATRIST

Sandra Kaplan provided mental health services to abused children at the North Shore University Hospital in Manhasset, New York, where she concentrated on the problems of physically abused adolescents.

HEATHER KEENAN, PEDIATRICIAN

Heather Keenan first became qualified in pediatric critical care at the University of North Carolina, and with Desmond Runyan's inspiration, she began to carry out research regarding the inflicted injuries of young children. This led to the first population-based study of the incidence of severe, inflicted head injuries, a landmark study.[2] Keenan then migrated to the University of Utah, where she continues to conduct research about child abuse.

RUTH KEMPE, PSYCHIATRIST

Ruth Kempe was educated in psychiatry and married C. Henry Kempe early in both of their careers. In addition to providing lifelong support to him and raising 5 daughters, she made substantial contributions to the care of abused children. She focused on the rehabilitation of infants and children who had been neglected or abused and who had developmental problems. She organized special childcare for these high-risk children and provided them with supportive therapy.

Along with Mary Edna Helfer and Richard Krugman, she co-edited the fifth edition of the famous text, *The Battered Child*. In addition, she wrote about infants and children with developmental problems related to neglect. She died as this book was being completed.

ROBERT KIRSCHNER, PATHOLOGIST

Robert Kirschner first published an article about child abuse in 1985.[3] In it, he described cases of injury deaths, which had been mistaken for abuse, but were in fact either unintentional injuries or postmortem changes that were not due to injury. In 1997, he wrote the chapters on the pathology of child abuse for the fifth edition of *The Battered Child* and for the first edition of Robert Reece's text, *Child Abuse: Medical Diagnosis and Management*.

Throughout most of his career, Kirschner was a member of the faculty of the University of Chicago School of Medicine, and he worked in the Cook County Chicago Medical Examiner's Office. He inspired many other physicians to work in the field of child abuse, including Jill Glick. Best known for his work in human rights, Kirschner's work helped convict officials from the former Yugoslavia and Rwanda of genocide in cases heard by United Nations International Criminal Tribunals. In 1994, he used DNA testing to identify the biological parents of children from El Salvador who had been kidnapped by the army during that country's civil war, sent to orphanages in the US, and adopted by American families. His examination in 1996 of 4 mass grave sites near the Bosnian town of Srebrenica, where about 8000 Muslim men and boys were thought to have been slaughtered by Serbs, contributed to the 2001 conviction of Gen. Radislav Krstic by the International Tribunal in the Hague on charges of genocide. From 1985 to 2000, he took part in 36 international missions to investigate suspected killings and human rights violations in many countries on behalf of organizations, including Physicians for Human Rights, the Organization of American States, the United Nations and its international tribunals, and the American Association for the Advancement of Science. His interest in child abuse grew from his convictions about human rights. Kirschner died at the early age of 61 while still actively involved in child abuse work.

HENRY KROUS, PEDIATRIC PATHOLOGIST

Henry Krous studied pediatric pathology at the University of Washington in Seattle with Bruce Beckwith, from whom he acquired a lifelong interest in what is now known as sudden infant death syndrome (SIDS). While performing his military service at the Naval Hospital in San Diego, he worked in the San Diego County coroner's office, performing autopsies on suspicious deaths, which exposed him to forensic pathology.

Krous became a leading researcher in pediatric pathology with many publications and an emphasis on SIDS. Since some apparent SIDS cases are actually cases of suffocation, an interest in sudden unexpected death naturally leads to an interest in child abuse. A number of Krous' publications deal specifically with child abuse issues.

RICHARD KRUGMAN, PEDIATRICIAN

While attending New York University School of Medicine, Richard Krugman heard a lecture by Kempe and was captivated by the man and the subject of child abuse. He was astonished first by the ugly facts of abuse and then by the bewildering capability of professionals in health and social services to see indicators of the problem in children and parents and do nothing about it. He entered a pediatric residency at the University of Colorado and continued to be influenced by Kempe.

Krugman performed his government service with the US Public Health Service and studied government in greater depth as a Robert Wood Johnson fellow, working in the office of Minnesota Senator David Durenberger. After Kempe retired, Krugman returned to Colorado as a pediatric faculty member and the director of the Kempe Center.

Krugman was an active child abuse pediatrician for many years and published extensively, serving as managing editor of the journal *Child Abuse and Neglect* for 15 years. He headed the US Advisory Board on Child Abuse and Neglect from 1988-1991 and participated in the writing of the 5 reports mentioned in *Chapter 6*. Although the recommendations of these reports were not acted upon quickly, they still carry great authority and, with some updating, could be used for policy development.

Having held many administrative posts at the University of Colorado, Krugman was ultimately appointed dean of the medical school and vice chancellor for health affairs. He has also served as the chair of the Association of American Medical Colleges (AAMC) and the chair of the Council of Deans of the AAMC (2001-2002) and is a member of the Institute of Medicine of the National Academy of Sciences.

In all of his positions, Krugman has labored to make child abuse medicine an important part of the national medical effort.

CYNTHIA KUELBS, PEDIATRICIAN

Cynthia Kuelbs completed a residency in pediatrics at the Rady Children's Hospital and Health Center in San Diego, California. She went on to the chief residency, and around 1980, began to provide care at the Center for Child Protection in the Children's Hospital. She acquired knowledge, skill, and experience in all forms of child maltreatment. After the retirement of this author in 1997, Kuelbs was appointed the medical director of the Center, later renamed the Chadwick Center for Children and Families. In that capacity, she headed up a medical team that provides services to a large volume of children that have been abused in a variety of ways.

In 2008, Kuelbs collaborated on a study of a large number of children who have experienced drowning or near drowning and demonstrated that hypoxia and ischemia of the brain, without mechanical injury, does not produce bleeding inside the skull,[4] an important forensic medical observation.

JOHN LEVENTHAL, PEDIATRICIAN

John Leventhal migrated from developmental pediatrics to the specialty of child abuse. During a distinguished career at the Yale

Medical School and the Yale New Haven Children's Hospital, he has contributed prolifically to child abuse medical literature.[5,6] For a number of years, he edited *Child Abuse and Neglect, The International Journal.* He also provided distinguished assistance to the definition and requirements for the new subspecialty of child abuse pediatrics.

ALEX LEVIN, PEDIATRICIAN AND OPHTHALMOLOGIST

During a pediatric residency at the Children's Hospital of Philadelphia, Alex Levin was influenced by Stephen Ludwig to take an interest in child abuse, and this started him on the path to becoming recognized as the leading doctor on ocular manifestations of child abuse. This topic is of great importance because one of the most dangerous forms of physical abuse, shaken baby syndrome, is often characterized by the presence of extensive retinal hemorrhages. A complete examination of the retina requires the use of a challenging technique called indirect retinoscopy, and skilled use of this technique requires prolonged training, which is usually not accomplished by doctors other than ophthalmologists.

After a residency at the Hospital for Sick Children in Toronto, Levin became board-certified in pediatrics and ophthalmology and served on the staff, providing eye examinations for hundreds of abused children. He also conducted research there, which has contributed significantly to the ability to distinguish abusive head injuries from accidental head injuries, with many publications on this subject. He is a gifted speaker and writer and has had a major influence on the field. In 2008, Levin returned to Philadelphia, where he continues his work in child abuse pediatric ophthalmology.

CAROLYN LEVITT, PEDIATRICIAN

Carolyn Levitt **(Figure 15-2)** is the founder and director of the Midwest Children's Resource Center of Children's Hospitals and Clinics of Minnesota, a diagnostic and treatment facility for victims of child abuse founded in 1986. Levitt has been the physician consultant to the Ramsey County, Minnesota Child Abuse Team since 1972 and was elected to the Executive Committee of SOCAN in 1988 and served for 6 years. As chair of the Education Committee of

Figure 15-2

SOCAN, she developed and edited the first edition of *AAP: A Guide to References and Resources in Child Abuse and Neglect* and co-edited the second edition.

Levitt was appointed to the AAP's Committee on Child Abuse and Neglect (COCAN) in 1989 and served through 1996. During that time, she was the lead author for the 1993 statement "Shaken Baby Syndrome: Inflicted Cerebral Trauma" and made major contributions to the 1991 AAP statement, "Guidelines for the Evaluation of

Sexual Abuse of Children," and to the 1999 revision. She has published extensively.

As a founding member of the American Professional Society on the Abuse of Children (APSAC), Levitt has served 3 years on the APSAC Board. She became involved early in the development of a system of child advocacy centers emanating from Huntsville, Alabama and Bud Cramer (see *Chapter 6*), and she established the first hospital-based child advocacy center. Levitt was a prime mover in the national initiative to establish health science as a leadership discipline in dealing with child maltreatment.

STEPHEN LUDWIG, EMERGENCY PEDIATRICIAN

Figure 15-3

While a third-year medical student in Philadelphia, Stephen Ludwig **(Figure 15-3)** first learned that child abuse constitutes a medical problem after listening to a lecture by Ray E. Helfer. During his residency at the Children's Hospital National Medical Center in Washington, DC, Ludwig began to encounter child abuse cases, but there were few guidelines available for dealing with them. Consciousness of child abuse was dawning in the hospital at that time (see *Chapter 4*). Being in Washington made it possible for Ludwig to be in contact with Senator Walter Mondale's staff, who were writing the Child Abuse Prevention and Treatment Act of 1974.

After completing his pediatric residency, Ludwig returned to Philadelphia and launched a new specialty of pediatric emergency medicine, while heading the emergency department at the Children's Hospital of Philadelphia. From this experience, he acquired knowledge and skill helpful in developing the new specialty of child abuse pediatrics.

Ludwig's reviewed publications cover a wide range of serious medical conditions resulting from physical abuse, sexual abuse, and neglect and commonly treated in hospital emergency departments. He has written about shaken baby syndrome, the effects of stairway falls, bathtub drowning, and other forms of serious and fatal inflicted injuries, including abdominal injuries and crush injuries of extremities. He has advocated for multidisciplinary management of suspected abuse cases and has defined the roles of prehospital caregivers, such as paramedics and emergency medical technicians. His mentoring and guidance led a large number of other outstanding physicians into the field, including Levin and Cynthia Christian.

JOHN McCANN, PEDIATRICIAN

In the early 1970s, John McCann left a private practice near Seattle to assume the position of chief of pediatrics for the Harborview Hospital, the county hospital for Kings County and Seattle,

Washington. His assignment was to establish and enhance a graduate program for primary pediatrics. Coincidentally in the same year, the Harborview Hospital established what was probably one of the first sexual assault centers in the US to provide services for adult victims of rape. McCann recruited Shirley Anderson to help him with the primary care program, and she developed the program for child sexual abuse in the Sexual Assault Center at Harborview Hospital.

Around 1980, McCann was recruited by the University of California, San Francisco (UCSF) Medical School to establish another primary care training program at the Fresno General Hospital. He carried out and published important work while in that setting. In his Fresno clinic for abused children, McCann saw a number of patients whose injuries occurred at known times, and he was able to describe the (surprisingly quick) healing of genital injuries in considerable detail,[7] which has proved immensely helpful in many cases.

By 1980, a number of medical doctors had begun performing examinations on children suspected of having been sexually abused. At that time, there was no published description that provided details of the normal genital anatomy of young girls, and only severe injuries could be reliably diagnosed as non-accidental. With the help of a psychologist and use of a survey instrument, McCann identified a set of young girls in whom the occurrence of prior abusive or accidental genital injury had been excluded, and he published the details of their normal anatomical findings.[8]

MARGARET MCHUGH, PEDIATRICIAN

Figure 15-4

Born, raised, and medically educated in New York City, Margaret McHugh **(Figure 15-4)** encountered and recognized child maltreatment early. In her school years, she worked as a weekend ward clerk at St. Vincent's Hospital in New York and met Vincent Fontana, who was already famous for his child abuse work. During her internship, she dealt with cases of physical and sexual abuse, and after she joined the faculty of New York University and settled at Bellevue Hospital, she established one of the first child abuse medical centers in the country with financial assistance from famous benefactress, Frances Loeb.

Older medical colleagues often asked McHugh why she was interested in child abuse, and she asked Kempe how she should handle such questions. His response was that she would need to wait for a generation of doctors to die. She did, and with some exceptions, they have.

Around 1980, when the AAP first established the COCAN to assist in development of policies and medical standards, McHugh became a member immediately. Over the years, large numbers of pediatric residents and, more recently, child abuse fellows have learned from her the ways in which doctors can do something useful about child abuse.

MARCELLINA MIAN, PEDIATRICIAN

While a junior staff member at the North Shore Children's Hospital in Salem, Massachusetts in 1975, Marcellina Mian dealt with the painful case of a 4-month-old infant with a fatal, inflicted abdominal injury and learned from the baby's devastated mother about the dynamics leading to serious physical abuse. Mian's mentor, William F. Rowley, helped her organize a hospital-based multidisciplinary team to deal with serious child abuse cases in Salem.

In 1980, Mian moved to the Hospital for Sick Children in Toronto to assist with its child abuse program. She wrote articles on various aspects of child maltreatment and was soon invited to join the Council of the International Society for the Prevention of Child Abuse and Neglect (ISPCAN). Through her work with ISPCAN, she became a co-author of the monumental international standard, *Preventing child maltreatment: A guide to taking action and generating evidence.*[9] This work sets out guidelines for any country that wants to address child maltreatment. Many countries have found the guidelines difficult to implement, and the moral status of children throughout the world still requires improvement. If this is achieved in the future, it will be due, in large part, to the work of Mian.

BRENDA MIRABAL, PEDIATRICIAN

Brenda Mirabal was recruited by a social worker to establish the first hospital-based child abuse team (Biopsychosocial Program for Battered Children) in Puerto Rico. During the last 22 years, the program has continued to receive Victims of Crime Act (VOCA) funds annually, and the interdisciplinary team has developed the competences to serve victims using evidence-based protocols with sensibility, dignity, and respect. Mirabal was drawn to child abuse work by the obvious needs of many children and the general lack of services. In addition to providing services, Mirabal has contributed substantially to new knowledge in the field.[10-12]

SAM MOORER, PEDIATRICIAN

Sam Moorer served in the Navy in San Diego in the 1970s and was influenced by John Schanberger, the chief of pediatrics at the US Naval Regional Medical Center in San Diego. Schanberger was very involved with the issue of child abuse and already had procedures in place for the recognition and reporting of cases that were seen in the facility.

After completing his military service, Moorer went to Tallahassee to practice general pediatrics and was soon invited by local children's services to provide medical examinations for children who social workers believed might have been physically abused. Subsequently, he was recruited by Jay Whitworth to head up the Tallahassee medical child abuse team. In this process, he was assisted and powerfully influenced by social worker Elizabeth Jackson, who left a senior position in public social services to join the health-based team conceived by Whitworth and led by Moorer.

ELI NEWBERGER, PEDIATRICIAN

Eli Newberger began his long career at the Boston Children's Hospital and the Department of Pediatrics at Harvard Medical School in the early 1970s. Always concerned with behavioral aspects of pediatrics, he gravitated toward the subspecialty of child abuse. A prolific writer and publisher, Newberger's early publications included an outrageous 1978 article in which he attributed the description of the diagnostic features of battered infants to the needs of pediatric radiologists to expand the scope of their field.[13] Not one to shy away from controversy, he often expressed concern about the way in which child abuse professionals exercised their power for intervention in child abuse cases. Newberger also pointed out the inequities in child abuse recognition and reporting that were connected to socioeconomic levels and to race.

RESMIYE ORAL, PEDIATRICIAN

Figure 15-5

Resmiye Oral **(Figure 15-5)** attended medical school and completed graduate training in pediatrics and preventive medicine in Turkey, and in 1993, she was contacted by the Turkish Medical Association's Human Rights Office and asked to join a task force on family violence. At that time, there were no medical child abuse programs in Turkey. The task force she joined quickly realized that, although child abuse was a form of family violence, it was sufficiently serious and prevalent to require a task force of its own. Also, child abuse was not seen as a medical problem at that time, but rather a concern for legal and social sectors only. At about the same time, ISPCAN established a chapter in Turkey, and Oral attended some of their meetings.

Through an American social worker, Oral got in touch with Nancy Kellogg in Texas, who sent her a box of publications on the subject of child abuse, which enabled Oral to educate herself on the subject. She then established the first multidisciplinary hospital-based child protection team at a hospital in Turkey. As a result, recognition of child abuse cases increased dramatically over the ensuing months. With this recognition came the realization that the abuse cases had been occurring for a long time but had not been diagnosed in earlier times. Oral was able to secure Turkish governmental funding to seek advanced training in the US, which she accomplished at the Columbus Children's Hospital and Ohio State University with Charles Johnson. Unfortunately, while she was engaged in this fellowship, the government in Turkey changed and the new Ministry of Health did away with the child abuse programs she had launched, retarding, for many years, Turkey's progress toward child abuse prevention. Oral then migrated to the University of Iowa to supervise a medical child abuse program. She has published a number of articles, some of which describe the situation of abused children in Turkey.

MORE STORIES

The next chapter will continue to detail the biographies of child abuse doctors.

REFERENCES

1. Jenny C, ed. *Child Abuse and Neglect: Diagnosis Treatment and Evidence.* Atlanta, GA: Elsevier. In press.

2. Keenan HT, et al. A population-based study of inflicted traumatic brain injury in young children. *JAMA.* 2003;290(5):621-626.

3. Kirschner RH, Stein RJ. The mistaken diagnosis of child abuse. A form of medical abuse? *Am J Dis Child.* 1985;139(9):873-875.

4. Rafaat KT, et al. Cranial computed tomographic findings in a large group of children with drowning: diagnostic, prognostic, and forensic implications. *Pediatr Crit Care Med.* 2008;9(6):567-572.

5. Leventhal JM. Twenty years later: we do know how to prevent child abuse and neglect. *Child Abuse Negl.* 1996;20(8):647-653.

6. Leventhal JM. The field of child maltreatment enters its fifth decade. *Child Abuse Negl.* 2003;27(1):1-4.

7. McCann J, et al. Healing of nonhymenal genital injuries in prepubertal and adolescent girls: a descriptive study. *Pediatr.* 2007;120(5):1000-1011.

8. McCann J, et al. Genital findings in prepubertal girls selected for nonabuse: a descriptive study. *Pediatr.* 1990;86(3):428-439.

9. Mian M. International Society for the Prevention of Child Abuse and Neglect (ISPCAN) and worldwide endeavors to prevent child maltreatment. *Child Abuse Negl.* 2004;28(1):1-4.

10. Mirabal B. [The interdisciplinary management of child abuse with respect to the law and the current treatment]. *Bol Asoc Med P R*. 1988;80(7):251-252.

11. Mirabal B, De Jesus H. [Early detection and cognitive rescue of abused children]. *Bol Asoc Med P R*. 1990;82(5):200-203.

12. Mirabal B, et al. Developing partnerships to advance youth violence prevention in Puerto Rico: the role of an academic center of excellence. *Am J Prev Med*. 2008; 34(3 Suppl):S56-61.

13. Newberger EH, Bourne R. The medicalization and legalization of child abuse. *Am J Orthopsychiatry*. 1978;48(4):593-607.

Chapter 16

Doctors' Stories: P-Z

As the previous 3 chapters have done, this chapter will provide the stories of child abuse doctors, all of whom are "early adopters" of the field.[1]

Doctors' Stories (continued)

The following entries are arranged in alphabetical order; therefore, the order of these doctors' stories is not an indicator of importance.

W. Martin Palmer, Pediatrician

W. Martin Palmer **(Figure 16-1)** was the grandfather of child abuse medicine in Utah. Before starting the Child Protection Team at Salt Lake City's Primary Children's Medical Center in 1975, Palmer was a general pediatrician. He led the state in the area of child abuse and neglect, providing expert medical consultation and teaching, a novelty at the time; leading the local multidisciplinary team; and developing the Child Protection Team into a regional resource.

Figure 16-1

He was active in the early efforts of the American Academy of Pediatrics (AAP) to improve policies and practices in the care of abused children and pioneered the field of child abuse medicine in the Intermountain West. Palmer died an untimely death in 1995 at age 62.

Vincent J. Palusci, Pediatrician

Vincent J. Palusci **(Figure 16-2)** received his medical degree from the University of Medicine and Dentistry of New Jersey and completed his internship and residency in pediatrics at New York University School of Medicine and Bellevue Hospital Center in Manhattan, where he was influenced by Margaret McHugh, who "infected" him with the need to care for maltreated children.

Figure 16-2

After 2 years at Bellevue as an attending physician in the child abuse, asthma, and pediatric tuberculosis clinics, Palusci joined the faculty of the College of Human Medicine at Michigan State University (Ray Helfer's department) and became a full-time child abuse pediatrician at DeVos Children's Hospital in Grand Rapids. While some questions regarding child abuse were answered, many new ones appeared, and he realized he needed tools for population-based studies. To do this, he earned a master's degree in epidemiology as a

TRECOS scholar at Michigan State. His subsequent work, which included developing groups for children exposed to violence, parenting programs for inmates and other at-risk families, child death review, and state-wide shaken baby syndrome–prevention education, was recognized in 2004 when Palusci was awarded the Ray E. Helfer Award for Child Abuse Prevention, given by the AAP and the National Alliance of Children's Trust and Prevention Funds.

Palusci was then appointed the Helppie Endowed Professor of Pediatrics at Wayne State University and medical director of the Child Protection Program at Children's Hospital of Michigan in 2005. He began the first child abuse pediatrics fellowship in Michigan and continued to teach medical students, residents, and fellows. In 2008, Palusci returned as professor of pediatrics to New York University School of Medicine and Bellevue Hospital's Frances L. Loeb Child Protection and Development Center to rejoin McHugh in the expansion of an innovative medical consultation program for caseworkers within New York City's Child Protective Services.

Palusci's publications address epidemiologic and health services issues for child abuse victims as well as the educational needs of general and specialist pediatricians. He serves on the editorial board for *Child Maltreatment* and reviews articles for *Pediatrics*, *Child Abuse and Neglect*, and other journals. He has edited 3 books, including *Shaken Baby Syndrome: A Multidisciplinary Response* with Steven Lazoritz and *Diagnostic Guide to Child Abuse and Neglect*.

FRANK PUTNAM, PSYCHIATRIST

Frank Putnam worked for 20 years in the Division of Intramural Research Programs at the National Institute of Mental Health before moving to the University of Cincinnati. He studied and published extensively on the biological and psychological effects of child maltreatment with an emphasis on the more severe abuse-related, clinical manifestations of dissociation and multiple personality disorder. In 1999, he became director of the Mayerson Center at Cincinnati Children's Hospital, which specializes in the evaluation and treatment of sexually and physically abused children and the development and dissemination of evidence-based prevention and treatment for child abuse, family violence, maternal depression, and related conditions. Putnam's work places him in the front ranks of doctors who have studied the ways in which child abuse affects the human mind.

ROBERT REECE, PEDIATRICIAN

Figure 16-3

Robert Reece **(Figure 16-3)** began his career in family practice and first encountered child abuse cases during a residency in pediatrics at

Boston Children's Hospital. He went to Cincinnati Children's Hospital as director of ambulatory services, where he participated in the child abuse team and returned to Boston City Hospital in 1974, where he was director of the Pediatric Walk-In Clinic (much like a pediatric emergency room). In that setting, a large number of child abuse cases were recognized and reported. At that time, Reece and Eli Newberger were the only pediatricians in Boston with an expressed interest in child abuse. With support from the Massachusetts Department of Social Services, Reece started a daycare center for confirmed cases of child abuse, and this program is still functional.

During Reece's tenure at the Boston City Hospital—from 1974 to 1989—he launched his prolific career, writing and editing child maltreatment literature. Although he is now associated with Tufts University and the Boston Floating Hospital, Reece has held appointments at almost all of the Boston medical schools and hospitals because of his expertise and prominence in the field of child abuse pediatrics. He has published articles with original observations about almost all forms of child maltreatment and edited books that have become standard child abuse texts in medical libraries. He originated *The Quarterly Update* and has continued to edit and publish this periodical, which reviews and summarizes child abuse medical research as it becomes available.

Lawrence Ricci, Pediatrician

Lawrence Ricci **(Figure 16-4)** first completed a pediatric residency and practiced pediatrics in rural Colorado, where all doctors were expected to provide all forms of medical service. He then completed a residency in emergency medicine, where he saw and provided care for both adult rape victims and sexually abused children. Both types of cases were not managed well in the early 1980s when he started his work.

Figure 16-4

Ricci had an early and disillusioning experience with the justice system in the trial of a suspected perpetrator of child sexual abuse. He learned that the courts needed to develop more concern for and knowledge about medical opinion. He set out immediately to improve the processes of diagnosis and care.

He then moved to Maine to practice emergency medicine in a community hospital, where he continued to be interested in the medical diagnosis of child sexual abuse as well as adult rape, and he introduced new protocols to assist in this process. In the early 1980s, the trickle of child sexual abuse cases that came into his emergency room became a flood, reflecting a national trend, possibly because of rising public consciousness of the problem.

Ricci used his growing clinical experience to publish a number of important observations and was able to emphasize the photo documentation of all sorts of abusive injury. Ricci became a member of the executive committee of the AAP's Section on Child Abuse and Neglect (SOCAN) and helped to build the educational programs for the AAP. Later in the 1990s, he joined with Cynthia Christian, Howard Dubowitz, Desmond Runyan, Reece, and others to launch the Ray Helfer Society.

Lucy Balian Rorke-Adams, Pathologist

Figure 16-5

Lucy Balian Rorke-Adams **(Figure 16-5)** began a pathology residency at the Philadelphia General Hospital in 1958. Because she was female, she was assigned to perform all the pediatric autopsies. After completion of the pathology residency, she advanced to a fellowship in neuropathology. The pathology department at Philadelphia General Hospital became the principal resource for the medical examiner's office for the city. From 1977 to 2004, Rorke-Adams was the neuropathologist for that office, where she consulted on most of the head injury cases involving children, especially those that were suspicious for child abuse. Her extensive experience in children's neuropathology resulted in many publications. In the 1990s, Rorke-Adams began to work with doctors who were associated with the Children's Hospital of Philadelphia and collaborated with them on a number of articles dealing with abusive head injuries.

Donna Rosenberg, Pediatrician

Donna Rosenberg worked at the Kempe Center in Denver for many years and contributed substantially to knowledge during that time. She had close connections to child abuse doctors in the UK and helped defend them from the attacks that took place there.

Desmond Runyan, Pediatrician

Figure 16-6

In the early 1970s, Runyan **(Figure 16-6)** enrolled simultaneously in medical school and the School of Public Health at the University of Minnesota. He was influenced by Robert ten Bensel, who pointed him toward studies of child maltreatment. Thus, Runyan became one of the few child abuse doctors with a master's degree in public health. When ten Bensel was disabled by illness, Runyan substituted for him, providing a number of lectures about child abuse at various sites. As a Robert Wood Johnson Scholar, Runyan completed a research project about decision making for foster children. He joined the faculty at the University of North Carolina School of Medicine and was soon appointed chair of the Department of Social Medicine.

Runyan's many publications about child abuse span more than 30 years from 1977 to 2009. They deal with almost every aspect of the child maltreatment problem, including diagnosis, forensic interventions, mental health ramifications, social context, and prevention. Runyan brings the powerful tools of epidemiology to the issue, and his contributions are uniquely valuable.[2]

JOHN SCHANBERGER, NAVY PEDIATRICIAN
John Schanberger was the chief of pediatrics at the US Naval Regional Medical Center in San Diego from around 1970 until his retirement in 1977. He was closely attuned to the problems of abused children, and he conveyed this interest to a number of pediatricians, who came under his supervision during their periods of naval service. He was instrumental in establishing a multidisciplinary team approach to child abuse in San Diego.

BARTON SCHMITT, PEDIATRICIAN
Barton Schmitt joined C. Henry Kempe's Department of Pediatrics at the University of Colorado in 1970 and was put in charge of ambulatory pediatrics at Colorado General Hospital, where he hoped to emphasize behavioral pediatrics. In that era, department chairs had the power to send their faculty members anywhere to do anything, and Kempe was famous for his delegation of important tasks. Within a month, Kempe had appointed Schmitt to the child protection team (without his consent), and the latter began to provide consultations for children suspected of being abused. In 1975, Kempe dispatched Schmitt (willingly) to Hawaii to assist the state in setting up medical services for abused children. The next year he was, again, dispatched to provide expert testimony in a landmark California case—*Landeros v Flood*—that established actionable civil liability for doctors who failed to report child abuse with resultant downstream injuries. Schmitt produced many valuable publications, including the 1987 article, "The Seven Deadly Sins of Childhood," which pointed out ways to prevent child physical abuse that still offer great promise. He wrote a chapter on physical abuse in 3 editions of the famous book, *The Battered Child*. His most notable contribution may have been a slide set with accompanying audio narrative that illustrated common types of abusive physical injuries. This set was sponsored by the AAP and has been kept up to date and is still available in the AAP bookstore.

SUZANNE SGROI, INTERNIST
Suzanne Sgroi's pioneering contributions are described in *Chapter 5*. As an internist at a private practice in Connecticut, she took a special interest in the sexual abuse of children and spoke and wrote extensively beginning in the mid 1970s.

ROBERT A. SHAPIRO, PEDIATRICIAN

Robert A. Shapiro graduated from medical school at the University of Illinois and completed a residency and fellowship in pediatrics at Bellevue Hospital in New York. He has practiced child abuse pediatrics for many years at the Children's Hospital Medical Center in Cincinnati and published extensively on a wide variety of medical issues in child abuse.

ANTHONY SHAW, PEDIATRIC SURGEON

Anthony Shaw **(Figure 16-7)** had completed residency training in pediatric surgery in the early 1960s when he was recruited by Vincent Fontana to join the Child Abuse Committee of the New York Medical Society. In 1964, he published an article about child abuse in a major surgical journal— a real rarity.

Figure 16-7

In 1970, he moved to the University of Virginia to establish a department of pediatric surgery, where he organized the first multidisciplinary, hospital-based child abuse team in Virginia. He contributed to the writing and enactment of Virginia's child abuse reporting law, and he served on the Governor's Advisory Committee on Child Abuse in that state.

In 1981, Shaw moved to the University of California, Los Angeles (UCLA) and practiced there until his retirement. In Los Angeles, he continued to provide consultation for child abuse cases and write about the subject.

ANDREW SIROTNAK, PEDIATRICIAN

Andrew Sirotnak was in a pediatric residency at the Wilmington General Hospital when he encountered a 5-year-old girl with a genital injury so severe as to require surgical repair. At the time he saw her, she was recovering from the operation, but there was still no explanation given for her injury. Despite the objections of the child's mother and grandmother, he interviewed the girl, and ultimately, she revealed the abuse by her grandfather. The difficulties in managing the case and in dealing with law enforcement, the justice system, and the family were daunting, but Sirotnak was motivated to look for better knowledge and migrated to the Kempe Center in Colorado for a fellowship. He has stayed on at the Kempe Center for about 20 years, becoming the senior clinical pediatrician, providing child abuse consultation at the Children's Hospital in Denver, and contributing substantially to new knowledge about child maltreatment.

DEMETRA SOTER, PEDIATRICIAN

Demetra Soter trained in pediatrics at Cook County Hospital in Chicago in the 1960s and soon concentrated her attention on pediatric trauma of all kinds, including mechanical injuries, drownings, and burns. Recognizing that child abuse caused many cases of serious and fatal injury, particularly in younger age groups, she joined the child abuse team at the Cook County Hospital and has continued her service there up to the time of this writing. Soter concentrates on clinical services rather than research, but she contributed to a textbook that correlates clinical and imaging findings in child abuse cases.

SUZANNE STARLING, PEDIATRICIAN

Suzanne Starling **(Figure 16-8)** was completing her pediatric residency in Greenville, South Carolina when she encountered a number of cases of abused children, without much instruction on what might be done. One of Carole Jenny's lectures convinced Starling that there was a specific medical approach to child abuse. She followed Jenny to Denver to a fellowship at the Kempe National Center and Denver Children's Hospital, and spent 3 years in Denver learning about child abuse and practicing child abuse medicine. It was during that time that she performed the research for her landmark study on confessions in serious head injury cases.[3] Many perpetrators stated that they had shaken the injured infant without causing an impact, some confessed to impact only, and some confessed to both impact and shaking. Most stated that the change in condition of the infant occurred immediately following the shaking. This was a very important forensic contribution.

Figure 16-8

Starling completed her fellowship in Denver and eventually settled at Eastern Virginia and the King's Daughters' Children's Hospital in Norfolk. She has continued to contribute to knowledge and educational processes in child abuse medicine.

BRANDT STEELE, PSYCHIATRIST

Brandt Steele's work focused on the histories and characteristics of parents of infants and children with serious inflicted physical injuries, rather than on sexual abuse, but he was the first psychiatrist after Freud to take a serious look at child abuse. He pointed out the absence of specific psychiatric conditions in the family members of battered children, emphasizing the generational nature of the problem and challenging the work of David Gil and others, who had argued that poverty was the most important contributing cause of child abuse. Steele pointed out that the Denver population of families, in which serious physical abuse had occurred, represented all economic and educational levels, while the studies of Gil and other sociologists focused on child welfare populations easily could have missed cases occurring in more affluent families.

Figure 16-9

JOHN STIRLING, PEDIATRICIAN

During a pediatric residency in Ann Arbor, Michigan around 1980, John Stirling (**Figure 16-9**) assisted in the development of a multidisciplinary team to deal with child abuse cases. He was also influenced by Helfer, then at Michigan State University, who also lectured in Ann Arbor.

Stirling moved to a private practice of general pediatrics in Vancouver, Washington, where the local child protective services workers discovered that he was willing to diagnose child abuse and provide medical services for victims. While in Vancouver, he came under the influence of Shirley Anderson and Jenny, who were building the program in Seattle. Stirling was able to provide services to a large number of child abuse victims, while still maintaining a highly successful general pediatric practice. This is a very difficult feat that has rarely, if ever, been duplicated. While doing this over a 28-year period, he also attended and provided instruction at many child abuse conferences around the country.

In 2007, Stirling left Vancouver to become director of a child abuse program at the Santa Clara Valley Medical Center in San Jose, California and a faculty member at Stanford University. Since making that move, he has begun to contribute articles for publication,[4,5] a task that was not possible in the busy setting of his private practice.

ROLAND SUMMIT, COMMUNITY PSYCHIATRIST

A published interview by David Corwin[6] describes the way in which Roland Summit became interested in child abuse. Summit's father was a school administrator responsible for guidance and child welfare. He shared accounts of his visits to chaotic families. Summit experienced painful empathy with abused children after reading the novel, *King's Row*, though he pointed out in his high school book report that a central theme of incest was too rare to fairly represent small town reality. His empathy for the characters of *King's Row*, as well as his father's vocation, contributed to Summit's desire to help people who had been abused.

As a medical student, Summit's ability to comfort patients in distress, especially in obstetrics and gynecology rotations, inspired him toward a career in psychiatry. The mentors in his psychiatric residency actually discouraged his concerns about abuse, pointing out that there was nothing that could be done about it. He chose to believe a young, suicidal patient's disclosure of incest, but was powerless to prevent her discharge back to her father's care (there were no child abuse reporting laws in 1957). Thereafter, Summit learned abuse dynamics from his patients, rather than from older psychiatrists.

Summit took a position as a community psychiatrist when that field was in its infancy. Community contacts led him to an appointment with Jolly K, who was promoting her idea of a self-help group for abusive parents. Summit was startled by the uncensored account of her sexual abuse history and its connection to homicidal impulses toward her daughter. As the founding board member of Mothers Anonymous (soon renamed Parents Anonymous [PA]), Summit heard from abusive parents' recollections they would never share in clinical evaluations, as well as a startling prevalence of child sexual abuse. Jolly K demanded Summit, despite his misgivings, undertake what would be his first written foray into that forbidden topic: the chapter entitled "Sexual Abuse" in the PA training manual.

In 1978, after several years of learning through painful experience and from persons who were victims and from consultations with social work and law enforcement agencies involved in child sexual abuse cases, he published a detailed description of various forms of intrafamilial sexual abuse of children. This was the era in which talk of child sexual abuse at professional conferences became possible. Summit was a gifted speaker, who could bring an incisive analytic capability to the discussion of this difficult topic, and he began to emerge as a major influence in the field. An example of his elegant analysis of child sexual abuse is from the 1978 article[7]: "The objective distinctions between loving support and lustful intrusion are disquietingly subtle."

Generally, the subtleties perceived by Summit were lost on the criminal justice system, or they were simply put aside by lawyers who could not explain them to judges or juries or chose not to, because they found Summit's findings disadvantageous to their clients and did their best to bury them. However, it was his article about the adaptations by child victims of sexual abuse[8] that led to the all-out attack on Summit by the cabal opposed to prosecution for child sexual abuse (see also *Chapter 9*). The article takes the reader into the mind of a young child to gain the child's perspective on the events of sexual abuse and the way it affects his or her life and familial relationships. It lucidly explains why children's accounts of abuse are often delayed, confused, and internally contradictory. Children seek ways to cope secretly with the abuse while still trying to protect vital family relationships, contradictory behaviors that typically leave adults confused and skeptical. When introduced in legal proceedings, Summit's explanation was effective in pointing out that the confusing statements of children were not an indication that abuse had not occurred. Later in a book chapter, Summit expanded the ideas from the accommodation article to describe the "exquisite fit" between pedophiles and their intended victims and point out the widespread societal "prejudice of innocence" for child abusers.[9]

Because his writing was forensically effective, Summit became a larger and more important target for the cabal that opposes child abuse prosecution. Some of his colleagues and associates were victims of damage suits launched by persons who had been adversely affected by their testimony. Ultimately, such conflicts were a factor in Summit's decision to retire when he still had much to contribute to the field. See *Chapter 5* for more on Summit.

ROBERT TEN BENSEL, PUBLIC HEALTH ACADEMIC

In the 1970s, the pediatrician Robert ten Bensel headed the Maternal and Child Health (MCH) program at the University of Minnesota School of Public Health, a position he used to network with community agencies. His prodigious energy and ability to speak effectively and persuasively made him one of the school's most effective ambassadors and made MCH one of the school's best-known programs. ten Bensel was one of few public health academics who considered the problem of child abuse important for public health work and published about it. He was responsible for launching Runyan into the field of child abuse medicine, blending clinical pediatrics with public health.

JAMES WESTON, PATHOLOGIST

James Weston gained his experience in child abuse while working in the medical examiner's office in Philadelphia. He wrote a chapter on the pathology of child abuse for the first edition of *The Battered Child* in which he notes the importance of pathologists' familiarity with the entire subject of child abuse. Weston emphasizes the importance of a prompt and thorough scene examination and interviews with all possible witnesses. He describes the techniques of autopsy as well as cases of physical abuse and neglect, resulting in fatalities. Written in 1968, Weston's chapter still stands as an excellent guideline for pathologists examining child abuse cases 40 years later.

JAY WHITWORTH, PEDIATRICIAN

Figure 16-10

The unique accomplishments of Jay Whitworth **(Figure 16-10)** are partially described in *Chapter 6*. In the 1970s, Whitworth was practicing pediatric nephrology at the University of Florida School of Medicine in Jacksonville. He began to take an interest in abused children and wrote about them as well. With substantial political assistance from Pediatric Department Chair Gerald Schiebler, Whitworth developed a vision for a statewide health service delivery system for abused children. Together, they worked over the next few years to make that vision a reality in Florida. In a short time, 21 hospitals sponsored multidisciplinary child abuse teams with support from the state's Department of Health Services, cobbled together from many different funding streams.

Whitworth published extensively about various aspects of child maltreatment, including his system for health services. He was still directing the program for Florida and providing leadership for the new field of child abuse pediatrics when he died suddenly in 2008.

HARRY WILSON, PEDIATRIC PATHOLOGIST AND MEDICAL EXAMINER

After qualifying in anatomic pathology, pediatric pathology, and forensic pathology, Harry Wilson settled in El Paso, Texas. He joined with Robert Kirschner to co-author the chapter on pathology in the first edition of the Reece textbook on child abuse.[10]

CONCLUSION

The experiences of child abuse doctors often included overcoming skepticism, indifference, and, sometimes, overt opposition as they pursued their important work. Doctors in the field of child abuse may continue to encounter some of these reactions as they work to prevent child abuse.

REFERENCES

1. Rogers EM. *Diffusion of innovations.* 4th ed. New York, NY: Simon and Schuster; 1995.

2. Runyan DK, Berger RP, Barr RG. Defining an ideal system to establish the incidence of inflicted traumatic brain injury: summary of the consensus conference. *Am J Prev Med.* 2008;34(4 Suppl):S163-168.

3. Starling SP, et al. Analysis of perpetrator admissions to inflicted traumatic brain injury in children. *Arch Pediatr Adolesc Med.* 2004;158(5):454-458.

4. Stirling J Jr, Amaya-Jackson L. Understanding the behavioral and emotional consequences of child abuse. *Pediatr.* 2008; 122(3):667-673.

5. Stirling J Jr. Beyond Munchausen syndrome by proxy: identification and treatment of child abuse in a medical setting. *Pediatr.* 2007;119(5):1026-1030.

6. Corwin DL. An Interview with Roland Summit. In: Conte JR, ed. *Critical Issues in Child Sexual Abuse.* London, Eng: Sage Publications Inc; 2001:1-26.

7. Summit R, Kryso J. Sexual abuse of children: A clinical spectrum. *Am J Orthopsychiatry.* 1978;48(2):237-251.

8. Summit RC. The child sexual abuse accommodation syndrome. *Child Abuse Negl.* 1983;7(2):177-193.

9. Summit R. *The Specific Vulnerability of Children, in Understanding and Managing Child Sexual Abuse.* Oates RK, ed. Philadelphia, PA: W.B. Saunders; 1990:59-74.

10. Reece RM, ed. *Child abuse: Medical diagnosis and management.* 1st ed. Philadelphia, PA: Lea & Febiger; 1994.

Chapter 17

ORGANIZING CHILD ABUSE DOCTORS

The trouble with organizing a thing is that pretty soon folks get to paying more attention to the organization than to what they're organized for.

— **Laura Ingalls Wilder**, from *Little Town on the Prairie*

Persons in the learned professions have tended to organize themselves into groups that can provide certain major, related functions. The first function is to provide mutual support to one another and an identity to the particular profession and, thereby, assure the welfare of its practitioners. The other major function is to establish professional standards and assure the welfare of the clients the profession exists to serve. Over time, many organizations have formed to fulfill these functions, and those that deal with child abuse will be the focus of this chapter.

SPECIAL ISSUES; SPECIAL NEEDS

Throughout this book, it has been made clear that child abuse medicine and child abuse doctors have not been welcomed with open arms by the medical profession or by society in general. As these doctors have looked for ways to organize their specialty, they have found some support.

THE AMERICAN ACADEMY OF PEDIATRICS

The American Academy of Pediatrics (AAP) was just 32 years old when C. Henry Kempe presented his battered child paper at its annual meeting in 1961. At that time, it was not the only pediatric organization in the US. Pediatricians in medical schools had been building the American Pediatric Society (APS) and the Society for Pediatric Research (SPR) as highly academic organizations for many years. The AAP was designed to provide a home for practitioners as well as academics and to deal with the practical, clinical issues of the health care of children. The pediatric, academic societies in that era would not have accepted the battered child paper for presentation and are just now beginning to show interest in child abuse.

At the time that child abuse became medically visible, the AAP had a committee in place that developed health policies about adoptions and dependency, usually involving children whose families had failed for one reason or another, leaving them vulnerable in many ways, but particularly for health. Issues concerning child abuse were referred to that committee for discussion and for considerations of medical policy. In 1979, this author was able to convince the AAP leadership that a separate committee on child abuse and neglect was needed, and the Committee on Child Abuse and Neglect (COCAN) was formed the following year. Richard Krugman was the first chair, and he ably headed the committee for the next 8 years.

A little later, the AAP also formed a Section on Child Abuse and Neglect (SOCAN) so that interested members could develop focused educational programs and communicate easily with one another. A listserv developed by Ann Botash of New York helped this group to come together. Thus, the AAP has been extremely supportive of medical efforts in child abuse and has endeavored to provide standards, as a professional society should. It is by far the most important medical organization that deals with child abuse; however, it does not always serve the needs of non-pediatric doctors.

THE AMERICAN MEDICAL ASSOCIATION

The contribution of the American Medical Association (AMA) to the development of child abuse medicine and the support of child abuse doctors has been intermittent and, in the long run, ineffective. A single committee meeting was organized in the late 1980s, and then, in 1995, the stars aligned, resulting in serious work that lasted for a few years. Robert McAfee, a surgeon from Maine, was elected president of the AMA at a time when the Chicago staff of the AMA included a crusading psychologist, Marshall Rosman. Both of these men had a major interest in intimate partner violence, and both were willing to include child abuse as a form of family violence, which could be included in an AMA policy process aimed at these important public health problems. McAfee and Rosman worked together to develop the AMA Advisory Council on Family Violence, and this council was established as an advisory group to the AMA Board of Trustees. It consisted of doctors, representing various medical specialties, with expertise in violence, including violence against children, intimate partners, elder persons, and other vulnerable populations. Child abuse doctors were included. An immediate, tangible product of this initiative was the writing and publication of excellent guidelines for medical management of the various forms of family violence, as they might present themselves to physicians.[1-4]

AMA presidents serve for a term of one year and are influential for about 3 years, after which they are expected to fade away. McAfee followed this course, and Rosman developed an illness and died prematurely. The loss of these enthusiastic founders has proved fatal for the AMA Advisory Council on Family Violence. At the time of this writing, it is poised to vanish altogether.

The AMA, as a whole, is having increasing difficulty in sustaining membership. Its tendency to lobby mostly for the welfare of doctors to the exclusion of the public health has cost the organization its credibility in political circles.

THE ACADEMY FOR VIOLENCE AND ABUSE

The Academy for Violence and Abuse (AVA) is a new organization being built from the "viable remains" of the AMA's expiring Advisory Council on Violence and Abuse.[5] This organization will incorporate most of the individual experts and health advocates that attempted to work with the AMA on health issues connected to violence of all sorts and particularly to child maltreatment. The incoming AVA president in 2009 is Robert Block, a child abuse pediatrician. There is real hope that the AVA can provide an effective health presence to deal with the social and political issues that impede substantial change and reduce the health effects of child maltreatment and other forms of violence. The AVA has taken the initiative with an excellent statement by Elizabeth Gershoff about corporal punishment based on earlier work[6] and summarized on their Web site.[5]

STATE AND LOCAL MEDICAL SOCIETIES

Many counties in every US state have medical societies, and most are considered constituents of the AMA. Some of these societies have supported child abuse committees; for example, the California Medical Association supported a child abuse committee for about 3 years around 1980, then abandoned it in the name of economy. The committee attempted to develop a regional plan for the health care of abused children that would assure access and quality throughout the state, but the parent association soon lost interest and withdrew support from the child abuse committee.

THE NATIONAL ASSOCIATION OF MEDICAL EXAMINERS

It was pointed out in *Chapter 13* that pathologists who are medical examiners are *ex officio* child abuse doctors, who regularly deal with child abuse cases whether they want to or not. The National Association of Medical Examiners (NAME) has produced a policy statement about a serious form of child abuse known as abusive head trauma[7]; however, NAME does not have a standing committee on child abuse. In fairness, it must be noted that the organization does not have any committees dealing with other specific causes of death.

THE AMERICAN ASSOCIATION OF NEUROLOGICAL SURGEONS

Neurosurgeons are often involved in the care of abused children with head injuries, but the American Association of Neurological Surgeons (AANS) has made a special contribution in the forensic medical arena. It is the only medical society of any kind that has disciplined a member for providing irresponsible expert testimony. This is a contribution to the child abuse field, because irresponsible testimony is common in litigated child abuse cases.[8]

THE AMERICAN ACADEMY OF CHILD AND ADOLESCENT PSYCHIATRY

A small minority of child psychiatrists are significantly involved in child abuse work, and the American Academy of Child and Adolescent Psychiatry contributes practice guidelines and medical policies for the field. For many years, David Corwin led the efforts of this specialty in dealing with child maltreatment.

MULTIDISCIPLINARY SOCIETIES CONTAINING DOCTORS

General recognition of child abuse has given rise to the development of multidisciplinary societies that attempt to deal with it.

THE INTERNATIONAL SOCIETY FOR THE PREVENTION OF CHILD ABUSE AND NEGLECT

Kempe and associates he recruited in the UK, France, and Switzerland founded the International Society for the Prevention of Child Abuse and Neglect (ISPCAN). Most countries of the world eventually joined. Child abuse professionals from all disciplines meet in congresses every 2 years and share knowledge and experience. The society publishes *Child Abuse and Neglect, The International Journal.* Over the years, ISPCAN has gained credibility at the United Nations, and its representatives, including Marcellina Mian, have contributed to the drafting of position statements dealing with children's rights and protections. Developing countries have always been active and welcome at ISPCAN, and their representatives have amply confirmed that poverty makes children vulnerable to abuse. This organization deals with topics such as child sexual abuse resulting from sex tourism, the sale of children, the recruitment of child soldiers, and the status of children in society.

THE AMERICAN PROFESSIONAL SOCIETY ON THE ABUSE OF CHILDREN

The concept of a multidisciplinary professional society devoted to child abuse was born at the "Summit Conference" in California in the mid-1980s. This event was organized by David Corwin (see *Chapter 13*). The first step was the founding of such an organization for the state of California, known as the California Professional Society on the Abuse of Children (CAPSAC). The national version, the American Professional Society on the Abuse of Children (APSAC), was founded about a year later at a New Orleans conference on child sexual abuse organized by Joyce Thomas. There was some sentiment supporting the idea that the organization should be focused narrowly on child sexual abuse, but a broader concept prevailed, and APSAC concerned itself with all forms of child maltreatment.

The American Professional Society on the Abuse of Children has thrived, and it holds annual meetings and has developed its own journal, *Child Maltreatment*. Along with the journal, APSAC has produced other useful publications as well as policy statements and practice guidelines. Most child abuse medical doctors are members of APSAC, although a large majority of members come from other professions, such as social work, law enforcement, or mental health services. The California Professional Society on the Abuse of Children has become a (California) state chapter of APSAC, and 10 other states have developed similar chapters with more in development.

JUST CHILD ABUSE DOCTORS: THE RAY HELFER SOCIETY

THE NEED AND REASONS

During the 1960s and 1970s, pediatric subspecialties began to emerge, mostly in response to exploding knowledge bases that made it increasingly difficult to provide excellent practice in all areas. The medical school departments and academic pediatricians dominated the subspecializing process, while practicing pediatricians tended to remain generalists. Subspecialization was codified and legitimized by the American Board of Medical Specialties (ABMS). Established in 1933, the ABMS, a not-for-profit organization comprising 24 medical specialty member boards, is the entity overseeing the certification of physician specialists in the US. The American Board of Pediatrics is a Member Board and oversees pediatric subspecialization. Generally, to qualify in a subspecialty, a pediatrician would need to extend the training period by 2 to 3 years.

In the 1990s, most of the pediatricians concentrating on child abuse work were connected to and supported by medical school pediatric departments or children's hospitals that were usually affiliated with medical schools. The idea of a formal subspecialty in child abuse pediatrics came naturally to these doctors. They were also driven by a need to prove expertise in qualifying to provide testimony in litigated child abuse cases.

One of the important leaders in child abuse pediatrics, Stephen Ludwig, had already developed another pediatric subspecialty in emergency medicine for children and had blazed a trail. The existing structures within the AAP, COCAN, and SOCAN were deemed insufficient for the task of creating the subspecialty. This may have been because the SOCAN had no academic requirements for membership but was open to any AAP fellow who chose to join and pay a modest additional membership fee. It appeared that a new organization of doctors was needed—doctors who would have conspicuous special qualifications in child abuse medicine and, perhaps, have made significant contributions to the development of the field.

THE FOUNDING PROCESS

The creation of this new organization was undertaken by Ludwig, Cynthia Christian, Howard Dubowitz, Desmond Runyan, and Lawrence Ricci. They organized and convened a meeting in Philadelphia at which the Ray Helfer Society was created, and the concept of the new subspecialty was developed in some detail. The meeting was attended by a representative group of senior pediatricians and a few other specialists who had contributed to the field of child abuse medicine. The need for the new society was not challenged, but there was substantial discussion about both the need for and the possibility of a new subspecialty. There was also a less-than-perfect consensus about the necessary duration of training. However, the process moved ahead, and the task of defining and gaining approval for the specialty was turned over to the AAP's COCAN. The committee chair, Block, became the point person who performed the bulk of the hard labor required for definition and approval of the subspecialty, which was achieved in about 4 years.[9]

NAMING THE SUBSPECIALTY

Deciding on a name for the new subspecialty was moderately contentious. The name "forensic pediatrics" would have been dead on arrival at the American Board of Pediatrics and was objected to on the grounds that it did not convey the broad and preventive approach to the problem favored by most pediatricians. "Child protection pediatrics" was rejected on the grounds it would cause confusion with the agencies involved in public social services.

Ultimately, the specialty was proposed and approved with the name "child abuse pediatrics."

GROWTH AND DEVELOPMENT OF THE HELFER SOCIETY

In 2009, the membership of the Helfer Society had grown to about 200. Medical doctors, who are recognized by peers as experts or leaders in the field, are invited to join following application with letters of recommendation from existing members. The criteria for membership have always been—and remain—vague as well as inconsistently applied. Although the Helfer Society membership is a little less than half that of the AAP's SOCAN, the superiority of the Helfer Society membership would be difficult to prove using any objective criteria, such as number of children helped, number of cases with expert witnessing, preventive services provided to families, or articles published. The Helfer Society has been able to organize excellent, scientific meetings, although with a rather small attendance, and it maintains a Web site.

POLITICAL EFFECTIVENESS

The AAP has an 80-year history of service to children and to pediatricians and, as a result, has a high level of credibility with federal and state governmental officials. Unlike the AMA, it has a reputation for putting children first, and its representatives are welcome in political circles. It maintains a Washington office and can often influence public policy in favor of improved children's health. The AAP is attempting to move a policy to improve support for child abuse medical centers. The Helfer Society has no political capability, and its members can only influence public policy by working through the AAP.

Many child abuse doctors have organized effectively, but a consolidation of the Helfer Society with the Section on Child Abuse and Neglect of the AAP would enhance the former's influence and efficiency.

REFERENCES

1. American Medical Association. *Diagnostic and Treatment Guidelines on Child Physical Abuse and Neglect.* Chicago, IL: American Medical Association; 1992.

2. American Medical Association. *Diagnostic and Treatment Guidelines on Domestic Violence.* Chicago, IL: American Medical Association; 1992.

3. American Medical Association. *Diagnostic and Treatment Guidelines on Child Sexual Abuse.* Chicago, IL: American Medical Association; 1992.

4. American Medical Association. *Diagnostic and Treatment Guidelines on Elder Abuse and Neglect*. Chicago, IL: American Medical Association; 1992.

5. Academy for Violence and Abuse. Academy for Violence and Abuse Web site. http://www.avahealth.org/. Accessed June 23, 2010.

6. Gershoff ET. Corporal punishment by parents and associated child behaviors and experiences: a meta-analytic and theoretical review. *Psychol Bull*. 2002;128(4):539-579.

7. Case ME, et al. Position paper on fatal abusive head injuries in infants and young children. *Am J Forensic Med Pathol*. 2001;22(2):112-122.

8. Chadwick DL, Krous HF. Irresponsible expert testimony by medical experts in cases involving the physical abuse and neglect of children. *Child Maltreat*. 1997;2:315-321.

9. Block RW, Palusci VJ. Child abuse pediatrics: a new pediatric subspecialty. *J Pediatr*. 2006;148(6):711-712.

Chapter 18

CHILD ABUSE DOCTORS IN THE FUTURE

The history of child abuse medicine and the activities of child abuse doctors have been described throughout this book. But medical doctors are not the sole owners of the problem. This chapter will attempt to visualize the future of child abuse work and will make the case that the health sector has the best chance of achieving substantial reduction in health harms caused by child abuse within a reasonable period of time and at an affordable cost.

PRESENT PRACTICE

PERSONAL HEALTH PRACTICE

Over the last 2 centuries, most medical doctors' contributions to this field have been in the form of observations of cases in which it could be determined that abuse had occurred; these observations resulted from the application of the principles of medical diagnosis. This is true of the work of Auguste Ambroise Tardieu, who described cases in great detail, and the later work of C. Henry Kempe and others in the 20th century, who expanded the descriptions of cases in which children were harmed by the activities of caregivers or other persons who overpowered them. This diagnostic process applied to cases fits within the definition of "personal health care."

At the present time in the US, there are a few hundred medical doctors who might meet the general definition of a child abuse doctor. These doctors mostly function as consultants in centers and provide medical evaluations for infants and children suspected of having been abused. They look at the physical injuries of infants and children and offer opinions about whether the injuries are accidental or inflicted by other persons. Child abuse doctors interview and provide medical examinations for children suspected of having been sexually abused, and offer opinions about what might have happened to those children. They often back up these evaluations with expert testimony in litigated cases.

Forensic medical diagnosis and documentation tend to consume a large fraction of child abuse doctors' time and energy. Many child abuse doctors also provide health services, including mental health services, to abused children, particularly foster children. Some also design and supervise child abuse prevention programs, and many carry out research aimed at shedding light on the diagnosis and prevention of child abuse. Mental health care for child abuse victims seems to have improved considerably in the last 2 decades, and a number of child abuse doctors who are also psychiatrists have led in this area, although most of the care is delivered by therapists who are not physicians.

PUBLIC HEALTH PRACTICE

Over many decades, medical doctors have suggested that public health has a role to play in the prevention of child abuse; however, the first clear statement about this policy took place in the fall of 1985 when US Surgeon General C. Everett Koop convened a conference in Leesburg, Virginia to develop policy statements about "public health and family violence," which included child maltreatment. Child abuse doctors were invited to that meeting, and the American Academy of Pediatrics (AAP) was formally represented. Koop spoke on this subject on other occasions and always acknowledged that child abuse was a "public health problem." Despite this pious pronouncement, most public health practitioners and public health academics continued to ignore child abuse. At the time of this writing, public health activity affecting child maltreatment remains infantile.

Currently, no state health department in the US has adopted standard case definitions for the identifiable health harms of child abuse, including child abuse death. No state health officer in the US could determine if the health effects of child abuse in his state had increased, decreased, or remained the same in the preceding 5 years. Adopting standard case definitions would be the first public health step. This failure of the nation's public health system to deal with child abuse despite a few top-down pronouncements constitutes a major, shameful, governmental policy failure sustained over many years despite competent, professional advice from such bodies as the National Advisory Committee on Child Abuse (see *Chapter 6*).

THEORY AND RESEARCH

COMPETING THEORIES OF CHILD ABUSE REDUCTION

For the last half-century in the US, the systems of public social services and justice have dominated the child abuse field and have received the bulk of public funding directed toward the child abuse problem. In that period, neither professional domain has discovered a way to determine reliably whether they are making progress or not. It is likely that there is less child abuse now in the US than there was a half-century ago, but this could not be rigorously proven. In fact, the scientists that support these 2 important sectors have not produced methods that can reliably measure trends or compare populations.

There appears to be a need in the US for a new political theory of childhood that would incorporate values such as children's rights and empirical knowledge of infant and child development, and the effects of external influences on the ultimate character, behavior, and health of adults. Along with incorporating the value of the protection of infants and children from defined preventable abuses, the theory should hold that the protection of children and the health of the public are closely connected and need to be served by persons educated about both personal and public health.

The Justice Theory

The justice theory holds that child abuse exists because of a widespread denial of the recognition of a child's right to be provided with care without the occurrence of any abusive caregiver behaviors. To a considerable extent, those behaviors can be (and have been) defined in law, and the violation of such law is a criminal offense and can be deterred and controlled by consistent punishment of offenders.

The justice theory has failed in practice for a number of reasons. The most important one may be that most of the abusive actions occur in private settings and are seen only by the actor and the child victim. Another related reason for failure is the requirement of proof beyond reasonable doubt prior to the imposing of criminal sanctions. Since almost all child abuse is unwitnessed, proof of occurrence depends on inference and circumstantial evidence or the testimony of children. These facts ensure the rarity of criminal sanctions. Also, most physically abusive acts affecting children are impulsive and unplanned, and it is clear that deterrence can affect only sexual abuse. Deterrence began only 3 decades ago when it was first recognized that child sexual abuse was prevalent. Still, the remedies provided by the justice system should not be abandoned. To ignore obvious injury and death of infants and children intentionally caused by their parents and caregivers would be unjust and demoralizing.

The Social Theory

The social theory holds that child abuse occurs because of social influences rather than individual aberrations in behavior. The influences are poverty and the accompanying disabilities of care-givers to protect their children or to provide for them properly and the general societal tolerance of violence as a method of control and education for children.

The social theory has had only limited success because no human society on earth has succeeded in approaching the elimination of poverty or economic inequity. While it is true that societal tolerance of violence affecting children may be abating and this, in time, will reduce child abuse, the inability of social scientists to develop rigorous and reliable methods for the measurement of child abuse remains a problem.

Social interventions present major difficulties in implementation because of extreme reluctance in a free society to the idea of governmental intervention into the process of child rearing. While it is obvious that the removal of the child from an abusive family can be lifesaving and very much in the child's interest, there is still much resistance to coercive social intervention in family life.

The Health System Theory

The health system theory for child abuse builds on the fundamental definition of abuse as something harmful. The harm of child abuse is harm to the physical, mental, and developmental health of infants and children that then persists into adulthood. Health harms are likely to be definable, measurable, and perhaps preventable by actions in health systems.

PERSONAL HEALTH VERSUS PUBLIC HEALTH

These 2 essential components of a health system are complementary, but they are competitive with respect to resources. In the particular case of child abuse medicine, it has already been noted that the initiative for this field has come from the personal health rather than the public health sector; however, personal health approaches that deal with one case at a time after a condition has occurred may have done all they can about child abuse. When conditions are advanced at the time of recognition, personal health remedies become expensive and less effective, and public health measures are needed. For example, tiny premature infants weighing about one pound at the time of birth can be saved from death by neonatal intensive care measures at considerable expense. Inexpensive prenatal care applied to large populations of pregnant women can reduce the incidence of prematurity to a small proportion. Developing countries wisely invest in prenatal care, rather than in costly neonatal intensive care.

There are many other examples of this problem, as it exists in health care systems throughout the world, but the message for child abuse medicine is clear—it needs to invest more in the public health approach. This change should take place immediately.

HEALTH-BASED PREVENTION IS PROMISING

Moderately successful programs for the prevention of child physical abuse and neglect have been developed.[1,2] They have accomplished this by providing home-visiting services by nurses working from health care settings. This method is not inexpensive, but it has the advantage of about 3 decades of carefully designed research and evaluation, and there is little question about its effectiveness.

Special attention and standard care to depressed or substance-abusing mothers in primary pediatric care settings also appear to reduce physical abuse and neglect.[3] This approach appears to be very inexpensive and deliverable through existing, primary health care services for children that are generally accepted by everyone. However, it is relatively new and needs more study.

The successful prevention of child sexual abuse in a population has yet to be described, although programs that instruct children about abuse[4] appear to be effective for improving case findings. Successful prevention of child sexual abuse may depend on the development of better knowledge about the motivations of abusers.

RESEARCH IS NEEDED IN ALL SECTORS

The theoretical considerations raised in the foregoing paragraphs imply a continuing need for rigorous research in health, justice, and social service sectors. This research priority should permeate federal sources of research funding, including the National Institutes of Health, the Centers for Disease Control and Prevention (CDC), the National Institute of Justice, and the Administration for Children and Families. Perhaps, the federal effort could involve a unique and groundbreaking cooperation and coordination between these agencies despite the traditional Washington view that such cooperation is an "unnatural act."

FUTURE PRACTICE

PUBLIC HEALTH AND PUBLIC HEALTH TARGETS

The future activities of the public health system affecting child abuse will be expressed in the following lists of targets or objectives. These represent the views of the author and are not derived from any sort of consensus process.

—The public health system at the federal level (the CDC) will develop standard definitions for the diagnosable health harms of child abuse and circulate them to the states. All states should adopt these definitions for the purpose of tracking the incidence and prevalence of child abuse. These definitions will be suitable for incorporation into the international classification of diseases (ICD). The definitions should also be developed in such a manner as to allow incidence comparisons among jurisdictions, detection of trends, and the study of interventions.

— The CDC will have the capability to publish reliable data about the incidence, prevalence, and severity of child abuse for each state and for the nation.

— Every state health department will employ at least one professional person, preferably a certified child abuse doctor, who will have responsibility for studying and managing publicly funded child abuse prevention efforts in the state. Cities or counties with populations of 3 million or more would employ similarly qualified professionals.

— Every state will provide programs for the prevention of physical child abuse and neglect, using methods that have demonstrated effectiveness and deploy these using maternal and child health services applied to populations that are having and raising children. Funding for these programs would be provided from Federal Title V grants to states and augmented with state-derived health funding.

PERSONAL HEALTH TARGETS

Child abuse medical centers offering an array of child abuse-focused services will exist throughout the US at a ratio of one center for every population of 3 million. These centers will be supported by federal funding, awarded competitively in 5-year increments.

— Research projects designed to determine why some adults sexually abuse children will be funded. The ways in which this knowledge can be applied to the prevention of child sexual abuse will also be determined.

— Health-based interventions that reduce the occurrence of pedophilia will be studied and applied.

— Primary health care services for children and families will include demonstrably effective prevention services for physical child abuse and neglect.

ACHIEVABLE GOALS

Although a specific quantitative timeline for the achievement of these objectives cannot yet be established, most of them could reasonably be accomplished within the next few decades. Fulfilling these goals will not create a perfect world for children and families, but rather a country in which maltreatment of children is being steadily reduced and the health harms of child abuse are abating. The process of change is being led by the health systems, while the support and attention of justice and social service sectors are maintained.

The goals and objectives are within our reach.

Health Care Reform and Child Abuse Doctors

At the time of this writing, the health care system of the US is undergoing reform for the first time in a century. In the past, the system grew to become inefficient, bloated, and inequitable with the result that it produced poor results overall for the public health, while incurring a cost so great that it could no longer be supported.

The process of reform offers an opportunity to increase the emphasis on health-based child abuse prevention and treatment. These changes might produce major reductions in chronic disease and disability, thereby reducing the overall costs of care.

THOUGHTS TO TAKE AWAY

Doctors of medicine first began to recognize the specific health harms resulting from acts of child abuse in the middle of the 19th century but few contributed to knowledge for that first century. In the mid-20th century, the stimulus provided by Kempe awakened medical interest first in the US and later in many countries. Now, in the early 21st century, it is possible to set out a rudimentary definition of a specialty called child abuse pediatrics.

In fact, medical specialties other than pediatrics are also contributing knowledge and skill to this evolving discipline. The major contributors are pathology, psychiatry, trauma and critical care, and emergency and family medicine. Child abuse doctors are to be found in all of these specialties, although they may not use that designation to describe themselves.

Doctors realized their unique knowledge and skill could be used to identify children who have been subjected to acts society would judge as abusive. It has also become apparent that medical doctors play important roles in the treatment of the conditions that result from abuse. Finally, but most importantly, it has become increasingly clear that medical doctors who understand public health may come to play an important role in the prevention of child abuse.

In the course of the development of child abuse medicine, doctors came to realize that they needed to work closely with social workers and with law enforcement officers and other professionals connected to governmental entities. Medical skills would often need to be applied to produce coercive interventions to interrupt ongoing abuse or to punish abusers. Because of these hard facts, the development of child abuse medicine has not been universally welcomed by society.

Medical testimony in support of possible criminal sanctions is almost invariably adversarial. The adversarial legal system also brings out the very worst that medicine can offer in the form of irresponsible medical expert testimony in many litigated child abuse cases. This does not mean that child abuse should be decriminalized. A concept of equal justice for children demands that harmful acts against them be treated in the same manner as harmful acts against adults.

Social interventions to protect children also require interference with family life and with family prerogatives in a way that offends many persons in a democracy. This does not mean that we should fail to intervene when the life or the health of a child is in jeopardy as a result of family failure. General improvements in prosperity seem to reduce child maltreatment, but are not easily achieved.

Hopefully, the future of child abuse medicine will see the field move in the direction of application of public health principles and epidemiology to the challenge of prevention of child abuse. A reduction in the necessity for criminal or social sanctions should be seen as prevention becomes effective.

REFERENCES

1. Olds DL. Prenatal and infancy home visiting by nurses: from randomized trials to community replication. *Prev Sci.* 2002;3(3):153-172.

2. Olds DL, Sadler L, Kitzman H. Programs for parents of infants and toddlers: recent evidence from randomized trials. *J Child Psychol Psychiatry.* 2007;48(3-4):355-391.

3. Dubowitz H, et al. Pediatric primary care to help prevent child maltreatment: the Safe Environment for Every Kid (SEEK) model. *Pediatrics.* 2009;123(3):858-864.

4. Wurtele SK, Miller-Perrin CL, Melton GB. *Preventing child sexual abuse: sharing the responsibility.* Lincoln, NE: University of Nebraska Press; 1992.

Handle any case of child maltreatment no matter what your discipline

The third edition of *Child Maltreatment* is the most comprehensive approach to identifying, interpreting, and reporting child abuse. This new edition is fully revised and updated with new contributions from leading experts in the field, making it the most complete resource available for addressing child abuse and neglect.

Facilitating a multidisciplinary approach to child abuse and neglect issues, the *Clinical Guide* has been expanded to 1000 pages and 43 chapters and addresses every possible facet of child maltreatment, including contemporary risks such as the Internet. The *Photographic Reference* has been updated with 850 new images, providing thorough documentation of physical abuse, sexual abuse, neglect, and crime scene investigation.

Child Maltreatment
A Clinical Guide and Photographic Reference
Third Edition
Angelo P. Giardino, MD, PhD, FAAP;
Randell Alexander, MD, PhD, FAAP

1749 Pages, 1925 images, 93 contributors
ISBN 13: 978-1-878060-85-3

$352.00

Quickly find information about medical aspects of child abuse when and where it is needed

For professionals working with children, the tremendous amount of information concerning child maltreatment can be difficult to retain. The completely revised and expanded *Child Abuse Quick Reference* is designed to provide these busy professionals with the information they need to recognize children at high risk for abuse and neglect and rapidly diagnose child maltreatment.

The chapters address the most common types of child abuse as well as uncommon but possible causes, such as cultural or religious practices that often look like abuse.

Knowledge is the best weapon against child abuse and this book helps elevate the understanding of those individuals working on the front line, making them better equipped to confront the challenges they face daily, and be instruments of positive change for the health and well-being of children and their families.

Child Abuse *Quick Reference*
Second Edition
For Health Care, Social Service, and Law Enforcement
Angelo P. Giardino, MD, PhD, FAAP;
Randell Alexander, MD, PhD, FAAP

448 Pages, 156 images, 93 contributors
ISBN 13:978-1-878060-60-0

$52.00

Quickly access information about sexual assault while on the front line

The *Sexual Assault Quick Reference* is an invaluable resource and field guide in a convenient pocket-sized format providing easy access to information for medical, forensic, and law enforcement investigations of sexual assault. Topics covered include the roles of multi-disciplinary teams, abusive and nonabusive variants, physical and forensic evaluation procedures, STDs, domestic violence, DNA collection and testing, disabled victims, and preparing for prosecution.

Sexual Assault *Quick Reference*
For Health Care, Social Service, and Law Enforcement
Angelo P. Giardino, MD, PhD; Elizabeth M. Datner, MD; Janice B. Asher, MD; Barbara W. Girardin, RN, PhD; Diana K. Faugno, RN, BSN, CPN, FAAFS, SANE-A; Mary J. Spencer, MD
560 Pages, 163 images, 69 contributors
ISBN 13:978-1-878060-38-9

$55.00

This text illustrates the problems of sexual assault and abuse through the eyes of many professionals, and the knowledge shared supplies others with the power to intervene. People in any related area can use this information to become empowered participants whose effective interventions help prevent sexual assault and care for its victims. Data are current, accurate, and specific to sexual assault, and the processes of detecting sexual assault, caring for victims, and prosecuting lawbreakers are thoroughly explained.

Investigate sexual exploitation anywhere with a pocket-sized reference

With an emphasis on 21st-century problems, this abbreviated version of the hardbound *Child Sexual Exploitation* is the perfect companion for all professionals who need a resource for combating child pornographers, leaders of child prostitution rings, and others who commit heinous crimes against children.

Child Sexual Exploitation
Quick Reference
For Health Care, Social Service, and Law Enforcement
Sharon W. Cooper, MD, FAAP; Richard J. Estes, DSW, ACSW; Angelo P. Giardino, MD, PhD, MPH, FAAP; Nancy D. Kellogg, MD; Victor I. Vieth, JD
384 Pages, 45 images, 52 contributors
ISBN 13:978-1-878060-21-1

$52.00

This user-friendly book examines different aspects of child sexual exploitation, including children victimized through pornography, prostitution, cyber-enticement, sex tourism, and human trafficking. Information on the medical implications for victims, how perpetrators of these crimes operate, and guidelines for successful prosecution and strategies for prevention, will empower those who seek to keep children safe.

Abusive Head Trauma
Quick Reference

For Health Care, Social Service,
and Law Enforcement

*Lori D. Frasier, MD, FAAP; Kay Rauth-Farley,
MD, FAAP; Randell Alexander, MD, PhD,
FAAP; Robert N. Parrish, JD*

355 Pages, 139 images, 32 contributors
ISBN 13:978-1-878060-57-0

$52.00

Investigate abusive head trauma using the best science available

Abusive Head Trauma Quick Reference allows readers to conveniently carry vital information into an examination setting. It contains all of the pertinent information on recognizing injuries, identifying children at risk, and implementing preventive measures, arranged in an easy-to-retrieve format for the professional who needs an immediate reference. In addition to assisting in a medical or social service setting, it also details the application of medical and scientific data to legal investigation and prosecution procedures. Addressing forensic investigation techniques and concerns, signs of intentional injury, findings at autopsy, and issues pertaining to providing expert testimony, *Abusive Head Trauma Quick Reference* details clearly the many considerations medical and scientific personel should bear in mind while performing a fatality review. *Abusive Head Trauma Quick Reference* is an ideal resource for any professional active in the fields of medicine, social services, education, law enforcement, or legal prosecution.

Child Fatality Review
Quick Reference

For Health Care, Social Service,
and Law Enforcement

*Randell Alexander, MD, PhD, FAAP;
Mary E. Case, MD*

350 Pages, 150 images, 73 contributors
ISBN 13:978-1-878060-59-4

$52.00

Essential and convenient guide for every member of your review team

The *Child Fatality Review Quick Reference* details information on how to start a child fatality review team in an area where none exist, and how to maintain and improve one currently in place. It contains a condensed version of the hardbound text, as well as brief case histories and additional charts and graphs for easy access to information. Child fatality review team members cross many disciplines, and those who will find this resource valuable include pediatricians, practitioners, Emergency Medical Technicians, radiologists, psychiatrists, pathologists, Emergency Room personnel, state and federal agents, judges, law enforcement personnel, safety personnel, child protection services members, attorneys, nurses, prosecutors, coroners, and medical examiners.

Full-color clinical photos illustrate abusive and accidental forms of death, including neglect, SIDS, suicide, burns, drowning, genetic diseases, and natural causes.